مستشارون حول الرسول ﷺ

Advisors of the Prophet ﷺ

© **Maktaba Dar-us-Salam, 2004**

King Fahd National Library Cataloging-in-Publication Data
Ash-Shanawi, Abdulaziz
Advisors of the Prophet. / Abdulaziz Ash-Shanawi. - Riyadh, 2004
176 p.; 14x21 cm
ISBN: 9960-9562-7-X
1 - Prophet's companions & successors   I - Title
239 dc   1425/4597

Legal Deposit no. 1425/4597
ISBN: 9960-9562-7-X

Printed in Lebanon

Advisors of the
Prophet ﷺ

Compiled by

Abdul 'Aziz Ash-Shanawi

Edited by

Abdul Ahad (Alig.)

DARUSSALAM
GLOBAL LEADER IN ISLAMIC BOOKS

Riyadh, Jeddah, Sharjah, Lahore
London, Houston, New York

First Edition: October 2004

Supervised by:

ABDUL MALIK MUJAHID

Head Office:

P.O. Box: 22743, Riyadh 11416, K.S.A. Tel: 00966-01-4033962/4043432 Fax: 4021659
E-mail: darussalam@awalnet.net.sa Website: http// www.dar-us-salam.com

K.S.A. Darussalam Showrooms:
Riyadh
Olaya branch:Tel 00966-1-4614483 Fax: 4644945
Malaz branch: Tel 4735220 Fax: 4735221
- **Jeddah**
  Tel: 00966-2-6879254 Fax: 6336270
- **Al-Khobar**
  Tel: 00966-3-8692900 Fax: 00966-3-8691551
U.A.E
- Darussalam, Sharjah U.A.E
  Tel: 00971-6-5632623 Fax: 5632624
PAKISTAN
- Darussalam, 36 B Lower Mall, Lahore
  Tel: 0092-42-724 0024 Fax: 7354072
- Rahman Market, Ghazni Street
  Urdu Bazar Lahore
  Tel: 0092-42-7120054 Fax: 7320703
U.S.A
- Darussalam, Houston
  P.O Box: 79194 Tx 772779
  Tel: 001-713-722 0419 Fax: 001-713-722 0431
  E-mail: sales@dar-us-salam.com
- Darussalam, New York
  572 Atlantic Ave, Brooklyn
  New York-11217, Tel: 001-718-625 5925
U.K
- Darussalam International Publications Ltd.
  226 High Street, Walthamstow,
  London E17 7JH, Tel: 0044-208 520 2666
  Mobile: 0044-794 730 6706 Fax: 0044-208 521 7645
- Darussalam International Publications Limited
  Regent Park Mosque, 146 Park Road,
  London NW8 7RG Tel: 0044-207 724 3363
- Darussalam
  398-400 Coventry Road, Small Heath
  Birmingham, B10 0UF
  Tel: 0121 77204792 Fax: 0121 772 4345
  E-mail: info@darussalamuk.com
  Web: www.darussalamuk.com

FRANCE
- Editions & Librairie Essalam
  135, Bd de Ménilmontant- 75011 Paris
  Tél: 0033-01- 43 38 19 56/ 44 83
  Fax: 0033-01- 43 57 44 31
  E-mail: essalam@essalam.com
AUSTRALIA
- ICIS: Ground Floor 165-171, Haldon St.
  Lakemba NSW 2195, Australia
  Tel: 00612 9758 4040 Fax: 9758 4030
MALAYSIA
- E&D Books SDN. BHD.-321 B 3rd Floor,
  Suria Klcc
  Kuala Lumpur City Center 50088
  Tel: 00603-21663433 Fax: 459 72032
SINGAPORE
- Muslim Converts Association of Singapore
  32 Onan Road The Galaxy Singapore- 424484
  Tel: 0065-440 6924, 348 8344 Fax: 440 6724
SRI LANKA
- Darul Kitab 6, Nimal Road, Colombo-4
  Tel: 0094-1-589 038 Fax: 0094-74 722433
KUWAIT
- Islam Presentation Committee
  Enlightenment Book Shop
  P.O. Box: 1613, Safat 13017, Kuwait
  Tel: 00965-244 7526, Fax: 240 0057
INDIA
- Islamic Dimensions
  56/58 Tandel Street (North)
  Dongri, Mumbai 4000 009, India
  Tel: 0091-22-3736875, Fax: 3730689
  E-mail:sales@IRF.net
SOUTH AFRICA
- Islamic Da'wah Movement (IDM)
  48009 Qualbert 4078 Durban,South Africa
  Tel: 0027-31-304-6883
  Fax: 0027-31-305-1292
  E-mail: idm@ion.co.za

Contents

'Abdullâh bin Zaid ﷺ

'Abdullâh bin Zaid ﷺ

His Full Name and Lineage

He is 'Abdullâh bin (bin means, 'son of') Tha'labah bin 'Abd-Rabbihi bin Zaid. He is from the clan of Banu Jusham bin Al-Hârith bin Al-Khazraj. Therefore, he is a Khazriji (from the Khazraj tribe) and a Hârithi (from the descendants of Al-Hârith). And he is also an Ansâri (title that was given to each native Muslim dweller of Al-Madinah; as opposed to a Muhâjir, which refers to a Muslim who migrated from Makkah to Al-Madinah).

His *Kunyah*

Kunyah is a kind of name, the form of which is, 'Father of so and so,' or, 'Mother of so and so.' It is often used literally for one's eldest son. So if one's eldest son is 'Abdullâh, one's *Kunyah* is Abu (father of) 'Abdullâh. But it is not necessarily the case that one's *Kunyah* is based on the name of one's eldest son, nor is it necessarily always the case that a *Kunyah* is used literally. It can also be used figuratively to connote a close relationship between a person and an object or idea. For example, since one famous Companion ﷺ was often seen with a small kitten (*Hurairah*, in Arabic), he was given the *Kunyah*, Abu Hurairah ﷺ. And if one wants to refer jokingly to the fact that his friend is wealthy, he might say to him, 'O Abu Fulûs (*Fulûs* meaning money).' Coming back to the point in question, 'Abdullâh bin Zaid's *Kunyah* was Abu Muhammad.

His Acceptance of Islam

After a number of years passed by without most of Makkah's inhabitants embracing Islam, a group of people from the Khazraj tribe of Al-Madinah visited Makkah and met with the Messenger of Allâh ﷺ at Jamratul-'Aqabah. Among the emissaries of Khazraj were As'ad bin Zrârah ﷺ, Râfi' bin Mâlik ﷺ, 'Uqbah bin 'Âmir bin Nâbi ﷺ, and Jâbir bin 'Abdullâh ﷺ.

"Who are you?" the Messenger of Allâh ﷺ asked them.

"We are people from the Khazraj," they answered. They of course knew the Messenger of Allâh ﷺ, or at least had heard of him ﷺ, for news of the conflict in Makkah was beginning to spread throughout the Arabian Peninsula. That news concerned the Khazraj in a most significant sense, for not only had they heard about the ongoing conflict in Makkah, but they also were constantly reminded by the Jews of Al-Madinah about the advent of a Prophet in Arabia. The Jews threatened them, saying that, when the awaited Prophet ﷺ appeared, they would follow him. And with him on their side, they would destroy the 'Aus and Khazraj tribes, the two native Arab tribes of Al-Madinah.

"You are allies of the Jews (of Al-Madinah)?" asked the Prophet ﷺ.

"Yes," they answered. A simple and true answer to a simple question; however, their answer did not fully explain the complex reality of life in Al-Madinah. In previous years, their tribe had constantly engaged in battles with the 'Aus tribe as well as with the Jewish tribes of Al-Madinah. But at the present, since there was no battle being fought, they could truthfully say that they were allies. However, the harsh reality was that the threat of war was always looming between the various tribes of Al-Madinah.

The Messenger of Allâh ﷺ then began presenting Islam to them. He ﷺ recited Verses of the Qur'ân to them, and they all listened attentively to his words. They were greatly impressed by the truthfulness of his tone and the goodness of his teachings. He was, they knew for certain, the awaited Prophet ﷺ that the Jews were always reminding them about.

"By Allâh, he is truthful," they said to one another. "He is indeed the Prophet ﷺ that the People of the Book have mentioned to us... and threatened us about, so do not let them beat us to him (i.e., beat us to becoming his followers)."

"You are indeed the Messenger of Allâh," they said to him. "We recognize you (from the description given to us by the Jews of Al-Madinah), we have faith in you, and we believe you. So command us, and we will not disobey you." They then told the Prophet ﷺ about the problems they were having in Al-Madinah and how the threat of war with the 'Aus tribe constantly threatened their safety. They ardently hoped that the Messenger of Allâh ﷺ would be able to unite the 'Aus and Khazraj and bring peace and stability to Al-Madinah. After this important meeting, the first Muslims of Al-Madinah returned to their hometown with the light of guidance.

13 years after the Prophet ﷺ received revelation for the first time, most of Makkah's inhabitants were still polytheists. To the credit of the 'Aus and Khazraj (and this was from the

grace of Allâh ﷻ),[1] Islam spread at a much faster rate among the dwellers of Al-Madinah. After the delegates of Al-Khazraj returned to Al-Madinah, they went to their families and informed them about their meeting with the Messenger of Allâh ﷺ. "O people," they said, "by Allâh, he is indeed the Prophet that the Jews warned you about, so do not let them beat you."

Whatever they had memorized from the Qur'ân, they recited to their people. The Verses they recited found a direct path to the hearts of their audience. One such audience member, 'Abdullâh bin Zaid ﷺ, immediately felt these words rolling off of his tongue: "I bear witness that none has the right to be worshipped but Allâh and that Muhammad is the Messenger of Allâh." Islam also began to spread among the 'Aus tribe. Before very long, the Messenger of Allâh's name was being discussed in every single household of both tribes.

A Return to Al-'Aqabah

Very soon thereafter, a total of forty men, some from the 'Aus tribe and some from the Khazraj tribe, began to perform prayer behind As'ad bin Zurârah ﷺ. These were all new Muslims, and they feared that the bitter wounds of the past would be revisited again. They feared that, because of past disputes, a man from the 'Aus would hate to pray behind a man from the Khazraj, or that a man from the Khazraj would hate to pray behind a man from the 'Aus. Wanting to avoid such conflict, 'Abdullâh bin Tha'labah ﷺ suggested that their Imam should be one of the Prophet's

---

[1] Reported by Ibn Hisham in *As-Sirah* 2/428 and Al-Bayhaqi in *Dala'il* 2/433, 435.

Companions from Makkah.

Since the idea made sense, and but they did in fact need someone to teach them more about Islam, they sent a letter to the Messenger of Allâh 鑅:

> 'Indeed, Islam has spread among us, so send us a man from your Companions who will teach us the Qur'ân, educate us about the ways and legislations of Islam, and lead us in Prayer.'

In response to their request, the Prophet 鑅 sent Mus'ab bin 'Umair 🍃 to them.

Then, in the matter of a single day, 'Usaid bin Hudair 🍃, Sa'd bin Mu'âdh 🍃, and all of the members of the Banu 'Abd-Al-Ashhal clan embraced Islam. One of the first tasks they set about completing was to completely destroy the idols that they had worshipped for their entire lives; and they did not hesitate in the least to do so, which was a strong indication of just how deeply Islam had penetrated into their hearts.[1]

One year after their previous meeting with the Prophet 鑅, a delegation consisting of 72 men and 2 women returned to Al-'Aqabah for a second meeting. This time around, 'Abdullâh bin Zaid 🍃 was one of the delegates. They chose 12 representatives to go and pledge allegiance to the Messenger of Allâh 鑅 on their behalf. And so the representatives went and pledged to worship Allâh 鑅, without associating any partners with Him in worship, and to protect the Prophet 鑅 just as they would protect their own lives, and the lives of their children and women.[2]

---

[1] At-Tabarani 20/362, Al-Majma' 6/41,42, Al-Bayhaqi reported in Dala'il 2/ 437.
[2] As-Sirah 2/459, Al-Waqidi 1/166 page 105.

The Call to Prayer

From the day the Prophet ﷺ arrived in Al-Madinah, one of his main concerns was to establish safety there, to extinguish the fires of enmity and hatred that had been raging for years between the 'Aus and Khazraj tribes. Things went well in this regard, for Allâh ﷻ united their hearts, and no longer was a dweller of Al-Madinah primarily known for being a member of the 'Aus or Khazraj tribe. Instead, every person who was a Muslim and a native dweller of Al-Madinah became primarily known by the title, *'Ansâri.'* The *Ansâr* (plural of *Ansâri*) were the native Muslim dwellers of Al-Madinah who welcomed and honored the Muslims who migrated from Makkah (these were the *'Muhâjirûn,'* or the 'Migrators').

Congregational prayer was quickly established; *Zakât* (obligatory charity) and Fasting were soon legislated, and so were the other laws of Islam. But in the early days that followed the Prophet's migration to Al-Madinah, the Prophet ﷺ led prayer when it was time to pray, but no announcement was made to notify the people that it was time for prayer. Preoccupied with business and other personal affairs, some people would miss the prayer.

Then, one day, the Prophet ﷺ consulted his Companions ﷺ about how they should gather people for prayer. Such a meeting was not an uncommon one, for the Prophet ﷺ would often consult his Companions ﷺ before he made a final decision in a matter. Allâh ﷻ said:

﴿فَبِمَا رَحْمَةٍ مِّنَ ٱللَّهِ لِنتَ لَهُمْ وَلَوْ كُنتَ فَظًّا غَلِيظَ ٱلْقَلْبِ لَٱنفَضُّوا۟ مِنْ حَوْلِكَ فَٱعْفُ عَنْهُمْ وَٱسْتَغْفِرْ لَهُمْ وَشَاوِرْهُمْ فِى ٱلْأَمْرِ فَإِذَا عَزَمْتَ فَتَوَكَّلْ عَلَى ٱللَّهِ إِنَّ ٱللَّهَ يُحِبُّ ٱلْمُتَوَكِّلِينَ ۝﴾

"And by the Mercy of Allâh, you dealt with them gently. And had you been severe and harsh-hearted, they would have broken away from about you; so pass over (their faults), and ask (Allâh's) Forgiveness for them; and consult them in the affairs. Then when you have taken a decision, put your trust in Allâh, certainly, Allâh loves those who put their trust (in Him)."[1]

One person suggested, "When it is time to pray, put up a flag. When the people see it, they can inform the others." This view did not appeal to the Prophet ﷺ. Someone suggested that, like the Jews, they could use a horn to announce the commencement of Prayer. Disliking this idea, the Prophet ﷺ said:

«هُوَ مِنْ أَمْرِ الْيَهُودِ»

"This is from the practice of the Jews."

Someone proposed that they use a bell. The Prophet ﷺ said:

«هُوَ مِنْ أَمْرِ النَّصَارَى»

"That is from the practice of the Christians."

Another person suggested that they light a fire: When the people see it, they will know that it is time for prayer.

«ذَلِكَ لِلْمَجُوسِ»

"That is from the practice of the Magians," said the Prophet ﷺ.

'Umar bin Al-Khattâb ﷺ then spoke: "Will you not send a

---

[1] *Qur'ân* 3: 159.

man to call people to the prayer?"

"I had indeed intended to send men out to call [people] when it is time for prayer," said the Prophet ﷺ.

«لَقَدْ هَمَمْتُ أَنْ أَبْعَثَ رِجَالًا يُنَادُونَ بِحِينِ الصَّلَاةِ، وَقَدْ هَمَمْتُ أَنْ آمُرَ رِجَالًا تَقُومُ عَلَى الآطَامِ يُنَادُونَ الْمُسْلِمِينَ بِحِينَ الصَّلَاةِ»

"And I had indeed intended to order men to stand on the rooftops of high buildings to call the Muslims when it is time for prayer."

The Prophet ﷺ then ordered Bilal bin Rabâh ؓ to call the people to prayer. Bilal ؓ stood up and called out, "The prayer is gathering (i.e., the Prayer is commencing)... The Prayer is gathering." People then began to issue forth from their homes and from the marketplace in order to pray behind the Prophet ﷺ.

'Abdullâh bin Zaid ؓ Sees a Dream About the *Adhân* (the Call to Prayer)

After 'Abdullâh bin Zaid ؓ finished praying, he returned to his house; he felt somewhat tired and wanted to go to sleep. When he tried to sleep, he fell into a state that was somewhere between wakefulness and sleep, or at least it felt that way. He saw a man wearing two green garments and carrying a bell in his hand. "O slave of Allâh, will you sell the bell?" 'Abdullâh ؓ asked.

"What do you wish to do with it?" inquired the man.

"Call (people) to prayer with it," answered 'Abdullâh ؓ.

"Shall I not guide you to that which is better for you?" asked the man.

"Yes."

"Say," the man instructed, *"Allâhuakbar* (Allâh is Most

Great), *Allâhuakbar; Ash-hadu Al-Lailaha illallah* (I bear witness that none has the right to be worshipped but Allâh), *Ash-hadu Al-Lâ ilaha illallah; Ash-hadu Anna Muhammadar-Rasûlallah* (I bear witness that Muhammad is indeed the Messenger of Allâh), *Ash-hadu Anna Muhammadar-Rasûlullah; Hayya 'Alas-Salah* (hasten to prayer), *Hayya 'Alas-Salah; Hayya 'Alal-Falâh* (hasten to the success), *Hayya 'Alal-Falâh; Allâhuakbar* (Allâh is the Most Great), *Allâhuakbar; Lâ ilaha illallah* (none has the right to be worshipped but Allâh)."

The man then moved away from 'Abdullâh 🕮, but not far away, and said, "And when the prayer is established (i.e., the *Imam* is ready, and the people are standing in the rows), say: *Allâhuakbar, Allâhuakbar; Ash-hadu Al-Lâ ilaha illallah; Ash-hadu Anna Muhammadar-Rasûlullah; Hayya 'Alas-Salah; Hayya 'Alal-Falah; Qad Qâmatis-Salah* [the prayer is established (i.e., the *Imam* is ready, the people are standing in the rows, and the prayer is about to commence)], *Qad Qâmatis-Salah; Allâhuakbar, Allâhuakbar; Lâ ilaha illallah.*"

'Abdullâh bin Zaid 🕮 then woke up in a very excited frame of mind. He remembered the dream so vividly that he thought he had been awake and not sleeping. He tried to control his excitement and let the matter rest until the morning. But as much as he tried, he felt that he couldn't wait, and so he 🕮 went to the Messenger of Allâh 🕮 and informed him about what he had seen.

"It is indeed a true dream, *In sha Allâh* (if Allâh wills)," said the Prophet 🕮, who then turned towards Bilal bin Rabâh 🕮 and said about him, "Let him make the call with (the words you heard in your dream), for indeed, his voice is sweeter and better than yours."

When Bilal ⬥ approached, the Prophet ﷺ said:

«قُمْ فَانْظُرْ مَا أَمَرَكَ بِهِ عَبْدُاللهِ بْنُ زَيْدٍ فَافْعَلْهُ»

"Stand, see what 'Abdullâh bin Zaid commands you with, and then do it (i.e., do what he says)."

'Abdullâh bin Zaid ⬥ began to dictate the *Adhân* (the Call to prayer) to Bilal ⬥, who proceeded to call out with it.

At the time, 'Umar bin Al-Khattâb ⬥ was in his house. If one could have seen him when the words of the *Adhân* entered his ears, one would have seen an expression of amazement on his face. He hurried out of his house and headed in the direction of the *Masjid*, and when he was in the presence of the Prophet ﷺ, he asked about the Adhan. In the discussion that followed, 'Umar ⬥ learned about 'Abdullâh bin Zaid's dream. 'Umar ⬥ then said, "By the One Who has sent you with the truth, O Messenger of Allâh, I have indeed seen a dream similar to the one that 'Abdullâh bin Zaid saw."

"All praise is for Allâh," said the Prophet ﷺ.

«قَدْ سَبَقَكَ بِذَلِكَ الْوَحْيُ»

"You have indeed been preceded in this regard by revelation."[1]

The people felt a sense of peace in their hearts when they heard the *Adhan* that morning; they came out of their homes and headed towards the *Masjid* in joyful moods.

With the Messenger of Allâh ﷺ

'Abdullâh bin Zaid ⬥ took part in the Battle of Badr and in

---

[1] *Abu Dâwud* 449 and *Ahmad* 4/43.

all ensuing battles. On the day of the Makkah Conquest, he carried with him the banner of the Banu Al-Hârith clan. And he performed exceptionally well during the Battle of Al-Hunain, displaying both bravery and skill in fighting.

A Narrator of *Hadith*

The following are some of the people who related *Hadith* narrations on the authority of 'Abdullâh bin Zaid ﷺ: Sa'id bin Al-Musayyib, 'Abdur-Rahmaan bin Abi Laylâ, and 'Abdullâh's son, Muhammad bin 'Abdullâh bin Zaid.

His Death

'Abdullâh bin Zaid bin Tha'labah ﷺ died in the city of the Messenger of Allâh ﷺ in the year 32 H, at the age of 64. The Leader of the Believers, 'Uthmaan bin 'Affân ﷺ, led his funeral prayer.

Sa'd bin Ar-Rabi' ﷺ

Sa'd bin Ar-Rabi' ﷺ

His Lineage

He is Sa'd bin Ar-Rabi' bin 'Amr bin Abi Zuhair bin Mâlik bin 'Imra' Il-Qais bin Mâlik bin Al-Aghar bin Tha'labah bin Ka'b bin Al-Khazraj bin Al-Hârith bin Al-Khazraj Al-Ansâri.

His Acceptance of Islam

Before migrating to Al-Madinah himself, the Messenger of Allâh ﷺ sent Mus'ab bin 'Umair ﷺ to Al-Madinah in order to invite its inhabitants to Islam. Sa'd bin Ar-Rabi' ﷺ was one of the people who embraced Islam at the hands of Mus'ab bin 'Umair ﷺ.

The Leader of Banu Al-Hârith

Sa'd bin Ar-Rabi' ﷺ was one of the delegates who traveled to Makkah in order to meet with the Prophet ﷺ one year after a smaller group had traveled to Makkah for the same purpose. This time around, the delegates said, "O Messenger of Allâh, take for yourself whatever you want, and stipulate for your Lord whatever you want."

He ﷺ said:

«أَشْتَرِطُ لِرَبِّي عَزَّوَجَلَّ أَنْ تَعْبُدُوهُ وَلَا تُشْرِكُوا بِهِ شَيْئًا، وَلِنَفْسِي أَنْ تَمْنَعُونِي مِمَّا تَمْنَعُونَ مِنْهُ أَنْفُسَكُمْ وَأَبْنَاءَكُمْ وَنِسَاءَكُمْ»

"I stipulate for my Lord *'Azza wa-Jall* (the Possessor of might and majesty) that you worship Him, without associating any partners with Him in worship. And (I stipulate) for myself that you protect me from the same things that you protect yourselves, your children, and your wives."

"And if we do that, what will we get?" asked 'Abdullâh bin Rawâhah ﷺ.

"You will get Paradise," said the Prophet ﷺ. After they expressed their joy at the opportunity of earning paradise, and after they said that they were ready to pledge allegiance, the Prophet ﷺ asked them to choose 12 leaders who would act as representatives on behalf of the others. They chose 9 people from Khazraj and 3 from 'Aus. From Khazraj, they chose Sa'd bin Ar-Rabi' ﷺ and 'Abdullâh bin Rawâhah ﷺ to represent Banu Al-Hârith (this and what follows are names of clans or sub-tribes); Râfi' bin Mâlik bin Al-'Ajlân ﷺ to represent Banu Zuraiq; Al-Barâ' bin Ma'rûr ﷺ and 'Abdullâh bin 'Amr bin Harâm ﷺ to represent Banu Salamah; Ubâdah bin As-Sâmit ﷺ to represent Banu 'Adi, Sa'd bin 'Ubâdah ﷺ and Al-Mundhir bin 'Amr ﷺ to represent Banu Sâ'idah; and As'ad bin Zurârah ﷺ to represent Banu Najjâr. From 'Aus, they chose Sa'd bin Khaithamah ﷺ and Rifâ'ah bin 'Abdul-Mundhir ﷺ to represent Banu 'Amr bin 'Auf; and 'Usaid bin Hudair ﷺ to represent 'Abdul-Ashhal.

The Prophet ﷺ said to these representatives:

$$\text{«أَنْتُمْ كُفَلَاءُ عَلَى غَيْرِكُمْ كَكَفَالَةِ الْحَوَارِيِّينَ لِعِيسَى بْنِ مَرْيَمَ، وَأَنَا كَفِيلٌ عَلَى قَوْمِي»}$$

"You are guarantors over (the) others, just as the Hawâriyyûn were guarantors for 'Iesâ bin Maryam.

And I am a guarantor over my Nation.''[1]

As'ad bin Zurârah 🙵 was the youngest of the representatives and the first of them to take the hand of the Messenger of Allâh 🌿 and pledge allegiance to him. For his part, Sa'd bin Ar-Rabi' 🙵 said, "I pledge to Allâh, and I pledge to you, O Messenger of Allâh, that I will not disobey you both or disbelieve in anything that you say."

Establishing Bonds of Brotherhood Between the *Muhâjirûn* and the *Ansâr*

It was important to unite the hearts of the 'Aus and the Khazraj, so that they could leave their bitter past behind them. And it was also important to bring the *Ansâr* (Muslim native dwellers of Al-Madinah, regardless of whether they were from the 'Aus or Khazraj) and the *Muhâjirûn* (Muslims who migrated from Makkah) closer together. Many among the *Muhâjirûn* had been rich, but when they migrated to Al-Madinah, they were forced to leave all of their wealth behind in Makkah; and all of the *Muhâjirûn* had left their homeland, the place they loved and called home their entire lives. And so in order to facilitate for the *Muhâjirûn* the transition of living in a new place and to unite their hearts with the hearts of the *Ansâr*, the Messenger of Allâh 🌿 established bonds of brotherhood between them. To each member of the *Ansâr*, he 🌿 assigned a brother from the *Muhâjirûn*. As for Sa'd bin Ar-Rabi' 🙵, his assigned brother from the Muhâjirûn was 'Abdur-Rahmân bin 'Auf 🙵.

"O 'Abdur-Rahmân," said Sa'd bin Ar-Rabi' 🙵, "I am indeed the wealthiest person from the Ansâr. I will give you

---

[1] Ibn Is-haq. See *Ibn Hisham* 2/446.

an equal share of what I have. I have two wives, and I will divorce one of them. When her waiting period ends, you can then marry her."[1]

"May Allâh bless you in your family and your wealth," replied 'Abdur-Rahmân ﷺ. It was a most generous offer from Sa'd ﷺ, and a most noble, dignified, and polite refusal from 'Abdur-Rahmân ﷺ, who then said, "Direct me to the marketplace."[2]

The Day of Badr

When the Prophet ﷺ gathered a small force to go out and overtake Abu Sufyân bin Harb's caravan – which was returning from Ash-Sham – Sa'd bin Ar-Rabi' ﷺ answered the Prophet's call and joined the other Companions ﷺ who went with the Messenger of Allâh ﷺ. During the battle that ensued, Sa'd bin Ar-Rabi' ﷺ fought both bravely and skillfully. A few years earlier, when Sa'd ﷺ was the representative of Banu Al-Hârith during the pledge of Al-'Aqabah, he vowed to protect the Prophet ﷺ. He certainly lived up to that pledge on the Day of Badr. May Allâh ﷺ be pleased with him.

The Prophet ﷺ Consults with Sa'd bin Ar-Rabi' ﷺ

The Quraish soon prepared another army to return to Al-Madinah; their goal was to exact revenge against the Muslims for the losses they incurred on the Day of Badr. Al-'Abbâs bin 'Abdul-Muttalib, the uncle of the Prophet ﷺ, quickly dispatched a letter to the Prophet ﷺ. The messenger

---

[1] *Al-Bukhari* 3780.
[2] *Al-Bukhari* 3780.

who brought the letter met the Prophet ﷺ at Qubâ. Upon receiving the letter from him, the Messenger of Allâh ﷺ handed it over to Ubai bin Ka'b ﷺ, who then began to read it to him: "Indeed, the Quraish has assembled an army to march towards you. Do whatever you see fit to do when they arrive. They have actually set out, and they are 3000 (fighters) in total. They are bringing 200 horses, and they have among them 700 armor-clad (fighters). Also, they have with them 3000 camels that are loaded with weapons."

The Prophet ﷺ asked Ubai bin Ka'b ﷺ to keep secret the contents of Al-'Abbas's letter. The Prophet ﷺ then entered Sa'd bin Ar-Rabi's house and said, "Is anyone in the house?" From the Prophet's tone, Sa'd ﷺ immediately perceived that it was a private or secret matter that the Prophet ﷺ wanted to discuss with him, and so he ﷺ said, "No, say whatever you need to say." The Prophet ﷺ proceeded to tell him about Al-'Abbâs's letter, intending thereby to seek Sa'd's counsel in the matter.

"O Messenger of Allâh," said Sa'd, "I indeed hope that there is goodness in that (i.e., for the Muslims to overcome them in battle)." Before they concluded their meeting, the Prophet ﷺ asked Sa'd bin Ar-Rabi' ﷺ to keep what they discussed a secret between them. After the meeting was concluded, the Messenger of Allâh ﷺ began the short trek back to Al-Madinah.

As soon as the Messenger of Allâh ﷺ left Sa'd's home, Sa'd's wife appeared and asked, "What did the Messenger of Allâh ﷺ say to you?"

"What does that have to do with you? May you have no mother!"

"I was listening to you," she said. She then repeated to Sa'd

ﷺ the entire discussion he had just had with the Prophet ﷺ. Sa'd ﷺ said, "Indeed, to Allâh we belong, and to Him we are returning!" He ﷺ then forced her to come out with him.

Sa'd ﷺ began to run, forcing his wife to move quickly along with him, until he caught up with the Messenger of Allâh ﷺ. "O Messenger of Allâh," he said, "My wife asked me to inform her about what you said, but I preserved our secret (and refused to tell her anything). Then she said, 'I heard what the Messenger of Allâh ﷺ said,' after which she repeated all that was said (during our meeting). I feared, O Messenger of Allâh, that news would spread because of that (i.e., because of her) and that you would then think that I had divulged your secret."

"Let her go," the Prophet ﷺ said. So angry was Sa'd ﷺ that he was still holding his wife by her hair. But upon hearing the Prophet's command, he forthwith let go of her.

The Day of Uhud

News quickly spread about the coming of the Quraish, and shortly thereafter the Prophet ﷺ and his Companions ﷺ – Sa'd bin Ar-Rabi' ﷺ included – set out for Uhud in order to meet with the enemy.

We know what happened next: the Muslims initially had the upper hand, and then a group of archers disobeyed the Prophet's command, which left the Muslim army vulnerable from behind. The polytheists then quickly took control of the battle, and the Muslims began to flee. It was at that juncture during the battle that Mus'ab bin 'Umair ﷺ lifted the flag of the Messenger of Allâh ﷺ and called out, "O people of Al-'Aqabah (referring to the Muslims who pledged to protect the Prophet ﷺ in the Pledge of Al-

'Aqabah), O leaders (referring to the leaders of the 'Aus and Khazraj who made the pledge on behalf of the others; Sa'd bin Ar-Rabi' 🙵 was one of them)."

Sa'd 🙵 heard this call and, without hesitating in the least, raced towards the heart of the opposing army, just as others were fleeing in the opposite direction. He fought valiantly, striking his sword at the many targets that surrounded him. But soon many fighters surrounded him, and it was only a matter of time before someone was going to deliver him a lethal blow. Yet despite his many injuries, he continued to fight with a great deal of zeal: his limbs were failing him, but his heart forced them to continue fighting. Then he fell down to the ground, though he still had some life left in him. No matter, though, for he had successfully fulfilled the covenant he had made to Allâh 🙵.

I Am Among the Dead

Around the time when Ibn Qami'ah announced that Muhammad 🙵 had been killed, Mâlik bin Ad-Dukhshum passed by Sa'd bin Ar-Rabi' 🙵, whose body was pierced in 12 different places.

"Do you know that Muhammad 🙵 has died?" asked Mâlik.

"I bear witness that Muhammad 🙵 has conveyed the message," said Sa'd 🙵. "But you must continue to fight for your religion, for indeed, Allâh is alive and never dies."

After the dust had settled from the Battle of Uhud and the Quraish had begun their return journey to Makkah, the first thing that the Prophet 🙵 said was:

«مَنْ يَأْتِينِي بِخَبَرِ سَعْدِ بْنِ الرَّبِيعِ؟»

"Who will come to me with news of Sa'd bin Ar-

Rabi'?"[1]

A man from the *Ansâr* stood up and said, "O Messenger of Allâh, I will go and see what happened to Sa'd, to see whether he is among the living or the dead." The man then went about the task of looking among the corpses and severed body parts that were scattered about on the battlefield. When he found Sa'd ﷺ, he saw that his body was wounded in many places but that he still had a few breaths of life left in him.

"What is your business?" asked Sa'd ﷺ.

"Indeed, the Messenger of Allâh ﷺ asked me to see whether you are among the living or the dead... "

"I am among the dead," said Sa'd ﷺ. "Convey greetings of peace from me to the Messenger of Allâh ﷺ and say to him, 'Indeed, Sa'd bin Ar-Rabi' says to you: May Allâh reward you for us with what Allâh rewards a Prophet for his nation.' And convey greetings of peace from me to your people... " After a few final words of advice for the Muslims, Sa'd ﷺ died. When the man from the *Ansâr* returned to the Prophet ﷺ and informed him about Sa'd's death, the Prophet ﷺ said:

«رَحِمَهُ اللهُ نَصَحَ للهِ وَلِرَسُولِهِ حَيًّا وَمَيِّتًا»

"May Allâh have mercy on him. Both alive and dead (i.e., on the verge of dying), he has been sincere to Allâh and His Messenger."[2]

Sa'd bin Ar-Rabi ﷺ and Khârijah bin Abi Zaid bin Abi Zuhair ﷺ were then buried in the same grave.

---

[1] Ibn Sa'd in *Tabqat* 3/396.
[2] *Al-Hakim* 3/200 and *Ibn Sa'd* 3/396.

The Two Daughters of Sa'd bin Ar-Rabi' ﷺ

Allâh ﷺ said:

$$﴿فَإِن كُنَّ نِسَاءً فَوْقَ ٱثْنَتَيْنِ فَلَهُنَّ ثُلُثَا مَا تَرَكَ﴾$$

"If (there are) only daughters, two or more, their share is two thirds of the inheritance."[1]

When this verse was revealed, Sa'd bin Ar-Rabi's wife ﷺ went to the Prophet ﷺ and said, "O Messenger of Allâh, Sa'd died as a martyr on the Day of Uhud, and he left behind two daughters." Accordingly, the Prophet ﷺ gave Sa'd's two daughters two-thirds of Sa'd's estate.

---

[1] *Qur'ân* 4: 11.

'Abdullâh bin Jahsh ؓ

'Abdullâh bin Jahsh ﷺ

His Lineage

He is 'Abdullâh bin Jahsh bin Ri'âb – Rabab – bin Ya'mar bin Sabirah bin Murrah bin Kathir bin Ghanm bin Dûdân bin Asad bin Khuzaimah Al-Asdi. His mother was Umaimah bint 'Abdul-Muttalib bin Hâshim, the paternal aunt of the Messenger of Allâh ﷺ.

His Acceptance of Islam

'Abdullâh bin Jahsh ﷺ was one of the early followers of the Messenger of Allâh ﷺ; in fact, he embraced Islam even before the Messenger of Allâh ﷺ chose Al-Arqam bin Abi Al-Arqam's house as the secret meeting place for the Muslims.

Al-Habashah

'Abdullâh bin Jahsh ﷺ migrated to Al-Habashah along with his two brothers, 'Abd bin Jahsh ﷺ and 'Ubaidullah bin Jahsh, and 'Ubaidullah's wife, Ramlah bint Abu Sufyân ﷺ.

Migration to Al-Madinah

'Abdullâh bin Jahsh ﷺ and 'Abd bin Jahsh ﷺ remained firm upon Islam; however, during their stay in Al-Habashah, 'Ubaidullah became a Christian and then died a Christian.

After a while, 'Abdullâh and 'Abd bin Jahsh returned to Makkah; they had perhaps been hopeful that the situation had improved for the Muslims in Makkah. But in this point they were mistaken; the Quraish's harsh treatment and persecution of the Muslims worsened, especially when they found out that the Aus and Khazraj tribes pledged to protect the Prophet ﷺ. When the situation became practically unbearable for the Muslims, they complained about their situation to the Prophet ﷺ. He ﷺ answered them,

«إِنَّ اللهَ قَدْ جَعَلَ لَكُمْ إِخْوَانًا وَدَارًا تَأْمَنُونَ بِهَا»

"Indeed, Allâh has provided you with brothers (i.e., the Ansâr) and an abode (i.e., Al-Madinah) where you will be safe."[1]

The Prophet ﷺ ordered the Muslims of Makkah to migrate to Yathrib, the city that later became known as Al-Madinah.

Fearing that the Quraish would prevent them from leaving Makkah, the Prophet's Companions ﷺ had to exit Makkah in a clandestine manner; and so it was for 'Abdulllah bin Jahsh ﷺ, his family, and his brother, 'Abd bin Jahsh ﷺ, and his wife Al-Far'ah bint Abu Sufyân bin Harb ﷺ.

'Abd bin Jahsh ﷺ was blind, but in spite of his lack of vision, he would always make circuits around the Ka'bah (*Tawâf*) without anyone's help. The morning after 'Abdullâh ﷺ and 'Abd bin Jahsh ﷺ left, the leaders of the Quraish became suspicious when 'Abd bin Jahsh ﷺ did not show up to perform *Tawâf* at his customary time. Abu Sufyân bin Harb was more troubled than the rest, since 'Abd bin Jahsh's wife was his daughter.

---

[1] *Al-Bidayah wan-Nihayah* 4/422. Reported by Ibn Is-haq in *Sirah* 2/468.

Abu Sufyân hurried towards Al-Far'ah's home, and upon arriving there, he found out that Far'ah ﷺ and 'Abd bin Jahsh ﷺ had already migrated to Al-Madinah.

Since 'Abdullâh ﷺ and 'Abd bin Jahsh ﷺ were one of the first Muslims to migrate to Al-Madinah, it was only after they left that Abu Sufyân became sure that the Muslims were secretly making their way to their brothers in Al-Madinah. And so Abu Sufyân went to Dâr An-Nadwah, where the leaders of the Quraish would meet to discuss important matters; there, he told the other nobles about his fears. They all decided that it was necessary to keep a close eye on the Prophet's Companions ﷺ and to prevent them from migrating to Al-Madinah. Their overwhelming fear was that the Muslims would become strong in Al-Madinah and then pose a serious threat to their trading caravans that had to pass through Al-Madinah (or at least near to Al-Madinah) on their way to Ash-Sham.

The Leader of the First Muslim Military Unit

'Abdullâh bin Jahsh ﷺ was one of the most beloved of people to the Messenger of Allâh ﷺ. Sa'd bin Abu Waqqâs ﷺ said, "The Messenger of Allâh ﷺ sent us on a mission and said, 'I will indeed send over you (i.e., send as a leader over you) a man who can patiently endure hunger and thirst more so than any one of you.' The man he sent over us was 'Abdullâh bin Jahsh, the first Amir (in this context, leader of a military unit) in Islam." Also, 'Abdullâh bin Jahsh ﷺ was the first Muslim to receive a flag for a military expedition.

He ﷺ was leading a military unit, but the goal of the mission wasn't to engage the polytheists in combat, but rather just to gather news about their comings and goings. This was necessary because, as soon as the Muslims migrated to Al-Madinah, the Quraish seized all of the wealth that they had left behind in Makkah. Even though fighting was not the goal of the mission, a skirmish did ensue, and the unit returned to Al-Madinah with two prisoners: 'Abdullâh bin Al-Mughirah Al-Makhzûmi and Al-Hakam bin Kaisân.[1]

Based on the spoils that they gained from their mission, 'Abdullâh bin Jahsh ؤ was the first to assign one-fifth of war-booty to the Prophet ﷺ, a practice that then became legislated with the revelation of this Verse:

$$﴿وَٱعْلَمُوٓا۟ أَنَّمَا غَنِمْتُم مِّن شَىْءٍ فَأَنَّ لِلَّهِ خُمُسَهُۥ وَلِلرَّسُولِ وَلِذِى ٱلْقُرْبَىٰ وَٱلْيَتَـٰمَىٰ وَٱلْمَسَـٰكِينِ وَٱبْنِ ٱلسَّبِيلِ﴾$$

"And know that whatever of war-booty that you may gain, verily one-fifth (1/5th) of it is assigned to Allâh, and to the Messenger, and to the near relatives [of the Messenger (Muhammad ﷺ], (and also) the orphans, Al-Masakin (the poor) and the wayfarer."[2]

'Abdullâh bin Jahsh's Sister Gets Married

Zainab bint Jahsh ؤ knew that she had certain qualities that made her more than eligible to marry any noble man among the Quraish. She was from a good family, with a good lineage, and she was very pretty. No one, especially not Zainab ؤ, would have thought, then, that she would end up marrying Zaid bin Hârithah ؤ, who was a freed slave. Zaid ؤ had entered into the household of the Prophet ﷺ as a slave, but then the Prophet ﷺ freed him and even changed

---

[1] *As-Sirah* 2/605, *Al-Bidayah wn-Nihayah* 5/36.
[2] *Qur'ân* 8:41. *Al-Majma'* 6/198 and see *As-Sirah* 2/601,602.

his name to Zaid bin (son of) Muhammad – though his name was later changed back to Zaid bin Hârithah ﷺ.

One day, the Prophet ﷺ proposed to Zainab ﷺ not for himself but rather for his freed slave, Zaid bin Hârithah ﷺ. Initially, 'Abdullâh bin Jahsh ﷺ was under the impression that the Messenger of Allâh ﷺ proposed to marry Zainab ﷺ himself. When 'Abdullâh ﷺ found out that he ﷺ was instead proposing on behalf of Zaid ﷺ, he rejected the proposal, based on the disparity in status between Zainab ﷺ, a free woman of noble lineage, and Zaid ﷺ, a man who was only yesterday a slave.

Soon thereafter, Allâh ﷻ revealed this Verse:

$$﴿وَمَا كَانَ لِمُؤْمِنٍ وَلَا مُؤْمِنَةٍ إِذَا قَضَى ٱللَّهُ وَرَسُولُهُ أَمْرًا أَن يَكُونَ لَهُمُ ٱلْخِيَرَةُ مِنْ أَمْرِهِمْ وَمَن يَعْصِ ٱللَّهَ وَرَسُولَهُ فَقَدْ ضَلَّ ضَلَٰلًا مُّبِينًا ٣٦﴾$$

"It is not for a believer, man or woman, when Allâh and His Messenger have decreed a matter that they should have any option in their decision. And whoever disobeys Allâh and His Messenger, he has indeed strayed in a plain error."[1]

When 'Abdullâh bin Jahsh ﷺ heard this Verse, he was overcome with feelings of sadness and contrition. He forthwith went to the Prophet ﷺ and humbly submitted to the command of Allâh ﷻ and the command of His Messenger ﷺ. 'Abdullâh ﷺ said, "Command me with whatever you want, O Messenger of Allâh, for by Allâh, I will not disobey Allâh and His Messenger. And I seek refuge in Allâh from the anger of Allâh and His Messenger." It is thus that Zainab bint Jahsh ﷺ was married to Zaid bin Hârithah ﷺ.[2]

---

[1] *Qur'ân* 33: 36.
[2] *Al-Majma'* 7/91,92, and Al-Qurtubi in his *Tafsir* 14/186 and see *Al-Bukhari* 4778.

Bonds of Brotherhood

When the Messenger of Allâh ﷺ formed bonds of brotherhood between the *Muhâjirûn* and the *Ansâr*, he ﷺ assigned 'Asim bin Thâbit bin Abul-Aflah ◈ to be the brother of 'Abdullâh bin Jahsh ◈.

The Messenger of Allâh ﷺ Consults With 'Abdullâh bin Jahsh ◈

The Battle of Badr was the first major military victory for the Muslims. Not only were many of Quraish's nobles killed during the battle, but also 70 members of Quraish's army were taken as prisoners. A decision had to be made concerning what should be done with the prisoners. At first, the Prophet ﷺ consulted some of his most trusted Companions ◈: such as Abu Bakr, 'Umar, and 'Abdullâh bin Rawâhah ◈. Among these select few was 'Abdullâh bin Jahsh ◈, which attests to his trusted position with the Messenger of Allâh ﷺ.

The Day of Uhud

When the Muslims, led by the Messenger of Allâh ﷺ, traveled to Uhud in order to meet with the enemy, 'Abdullâh bin Jahsh ◈ said to Sa'd bin Abu Waqqâs ◈, "Will you not come (with me), so that (together) we can supplicate to Allâh?" They sat down away from the others, and Sa'd ◈ began by saying, "O my Lord, when I meet with the enemy tomorrow, make me face a man who is very brave and strong, and who is severe in his anger. Then make me fight him for You and make him fight me. Then grant me victory over him, so that I will kill him and take his (things as) booty." 'Abdullâh bin Jahsh ⚔ said, "*Āmin*," after Sa'd ⚔ was finished with his supplication.

'Abdullâh bin Jahsh ⚔ then said, "O Allâh, provide me tomorrow with a man who is brave and strong and who is very severe when he becomes angry. Make me fight him for You and make him fight me, kill me, and then take me in order to cut off my nose and ear. Then when I will meet You, You will say, 'O slave of Allâh, for what (cause) was your nose and ear cut off?' Then I will say, 'For You and for Your Messenger (i.e., for Your Messenger's Cause, which is the cause of Allâh).' And you will say, 'You have spoken the truth.'"[1]

The Stick

When the two armies faced each other, Talhah bin Abu Talhah came forward with the banner of the polytheists in his hand. He challenged anyone from the Muslim army to come out and engage in a duel with him. 'Ali bin Abu Tâlib ⚔ came forward to accept the challenge. The duel did not last long, for 'Ali ⚔ quickly managed to deliver a lethal blow to Talhah.

Next, Talhah's brother, 'Uthmân bin Abu Talhah, came forward and issued a similar challenge. This time around it was Hamzah bin 'Abdul-Muttalib ⚔ who came forward to accept his challenge. With a swift and lethal blow to the head, Hamzah ⚔ brought down his opponent. Then Abu Sa'id bin Abi Talhah, brother of Talhah and 'Uthmân, came forward and issued the same challenge, hoping to exact revenge for the death of his two brothers. Sa'd bin Abu

---

[1] *Majma'* 9/302.

Waqqâs ؓ came forward to accept his challenge. When the duel began, Sa'd ؓ dealt such a powerful blow to right hand of Abu Sa'id that it instantly became severed from his body. Abu Sa'id then took the banner of the polytheists' army in his left hand, but almost as quickly as he did so, Sa'd ؓ cut off his left hand as well. With blood gushing forth from his two hands, Abu Sa'id clung to the banner with his two arms crossed, so that the banner was resting on his chest. Sa'd knelt down to his opponent and struck him through an opening he found between Abu Sa'id armor and helmet. After he killed Abu Sa'id, Sa'd ؓ began to take his armor as booty; thus was his supplication of the day before answered. After this final duel, the battle began in earnest. The Muslim army clearly had the upper hand, until the archers disobeyed the Prophet's command, as is well documented in the books of *Sirah*.

As for 'Abdullâh bin Jahsh ؓ, he continued to fight until his sword broke, at which point he went to the Prophet ﷺ, who gave him a stick that came from a date-palm tree. Once in 'Abdullâh's hand, the stick transformed, by the permission of Allâh ﷻ, into a sword.

His Supplication Answered

When the dust had settled after the Battle of Uhud, the Messenger of Allâh ﷺ walked through the battlefield, looking for the bodies of his fallen Companions ؓ. He ﷺ saw 'Abdullâh bin Jahsh's corpse, which was beside the corpse of Hamzah bin 'Abdul-Muttalib ؓ. Upon closer inspection, it became clear that 'Abdullâh bin Jahsh's nose and ear had been cut off. Concerning his fallen companion ؓ, Sa'd bin Abu Waqqâs ؓ said, "I indeed saw him at the end of the afternoon and both his ear and his nose were left hanging on a piece of string."[1] 'Abdullâh bin Jahsh ﷺ was truthful to Allâh ﷻ in his supplication, and so Allâh ﷻ granted him what he so ardently desired.[2]

'Abdullâh bin Jahsh's Death

Of 'Abdullâh's death it is known that he fought valiantly during the Battle of Uhud until his sword broke. Then he fought with Al-'Urjûn (literally: the stick), which the Prophet ﷺ had given to him. It had been a stick that came from a date-palm tree, but by the permission of Allâh ﷻ, it turned into a sword, thus becoming another miracle that Allâh ﷻ bestowed upon the Prophet ﷺ. Then 'Abdullâh ﷺ met on the battlefield a man who was brave, strong, and severe in his anger – namely, Abul-Hakam bin Al-Akhnas bin Shuraiq. And during the fighting that ensued, Abul-Hakam killed 'Abdullâh bin Jahsh ﷺ.

'Abdullâh bin Jahsh ﷺ and Hamzah bin 'Abdul-Muttalib ﷺ were later buried in the same grave. On the day that he died, 'Abdullâh bin Jahsh ﷺ was in his middle to late forties.

---

[1] *At-Tabarani* 9/301.

[2] *Al-Isabah* 4/32.

Salmân Al-Fârisi ﷺ

Salmân Al-Fârisi ﷺ

Salmân was from the people of Fâris. Originally, he was from Asbahân, and he lived in a town called Jai. His father was the leader of that town, and he loved no one from Allâh's creation even nearly as much as he loved his son, Salmân ﷺ. His love, however, was of the extreme kind. He didn't want Salmân to go out and see the world, fearing that some evil might befall him or that some evil change might come over him. Just as a father confines his beautiful daughter to her home, Salmân's father strictly forbade his son from ever leaving his house.

The people of Jai were Magians, people who venerated fire in honor of their deity of light. Perhaps out of loyalty to his father's religion, or perhaps because Magianism was the only religion he knew, Salmân ﷺ strived hard to be a devout Magian. It was he who would go to his father's kindled fires, making sure that they never became extinguished.

Being the leader of Jai, Salmân's father had many duties, both civic and personal. Among the things he owned were a huge field and a building. Normally, he would look after his field, but one day he had an urgent errand to take care of at his building. He had no choice but to ask Salmân ﷺ to help him: "O Salmân," he said, "I will be busy at my building today, so go to my land and take care of it."

"But don't wander about," cautioned Salmân's father. "You

are more important to me than anything else, and so if I hear that you are late, I will have to drop everything else and look for you."

The dutiful son that he was, Salmân ﷺ immediately set out for his father's field, probably for the first time alone. On his way, he passed by a Christian church, and he heard voices of people praying inside. He had no idea who these people were or who it was that they were worshipping, for as I mentioned earlier, Salmân ﷺ lived a very closed life, not being allowed to go anywhere unless accompanied by his father. Living such a closed life made Salmân ﷺ have the curiosity of a child, and so he entered the church to see what the people inside were doing. When he saw them, he was very impressed by their worship, and it was evident to him that their religion was more worthy to be followed than the religion of his father. "By Allâh, this is indeed better than the religion that we are upon," he exclaimed.

Salmân ﷺ got so caught up in the doings of the worshippers inside of the church, that he forgot about the field until the time of sunset. Being pressed for time, Salmân ﷺ asked the Christians, "Where is the source of this religion?" "It is in Ash-Sham (Syria and surrounding regions)," they answered.

Knowing that it was obviously too late to go to the field, Salmân ﷺ hurried home to his father, who, instead of working on his building, had been frantically searching for Salmân ﷺ the entire day. "My son, where have you been!" he exclaimed upon seeing Salmân ﷺ. "Did I not give you clear instructions?"

"My father, I passed by a group of people praying in a church," explained Salmân. "I was very much impressed by their religion. Then, by Allâh, I remained with them until sunset."

"My son, there is nothing good about that religion," Salmân's father tried to reason. "Your religion, the religion of your fathers, is indeed better."

"No," exclaimed Salmân 🕮, with a resolute tone in his voice. "It is indeed better than our religion." Salmân's father now became sure that he could no longer trust his son to be alone and that he would have to help him in spite of himself. Hence he decided to tie Salmân's leg to his bed and confine him to his home.

But Salmân Al-Fârisi 🕮 was determined and was not going to give up so easily. He managed to send the following message to the Christians in the church: "When a caravan comes to you from Ash-Sham, send news to me about their arrival."

Soon thereafter a caravan consisting of Christian businessmen did in fact arrive from Ash-Sham. The Christian worshipers inside of the church secretly sent news to Salmân 🕮 about their arrival. Salmân 🕮 responded with this message: "When they are finished with their business here and are about to head back to their homeland, send news to me about their departure." When they had finally sent news to him about their imminent departure, he managed to free himself from the chain that held one of his legs down. Having caught up with the traveling businessmen, he went with them to Ash-Sham. Once there, he asked, "From the followers of this religion, who has the most knowledge?" They directed him to the priest of the local church.

When Salmân 🕮 met with the priest, he said to him,

"Indeed, I want to be a follower of this religion, and I want to be with you. I will be as a servant to you in your church, and at the same time I will learn from you and pray alongside you." The priest accepted his offer and admitted him into the church.

Much to his disappointment, Salmân ☙ soon found out that the priest was an evil man. He would order his congregation to give charity, but instead of distributing what they gave to the poor, he hoarded their wealth for himself. He soon managed to hoard away seven containers of gold and silver. Salmân ☙ despised the priest for his evil actions, but he didn't have to put up with him for long, for he soon died. Upon the priest's death, the members of his congregation gathered to bury him. But Salmân ☙ put a stop to the funeral. "Indeed, he was an evil man," announced Salmân ☙ before all who were present for the funeral. "He used to order you to give charity, and he used to exhort you to give (to the poor), but when you came to him with money for charity, he hoarded that money for himself, without giving any of it to the poor."

"And how do you know this?" they asked incredulously.

"I will show you where he hid his treasure," said Salmân ☙. After Salmân ☙ took them to the place of the hidden treasure, they were all shocked to see seven filled containers of gold and silver. "By Allâh, we will never bury him," they exclaimed. They were true to their oath, for instead of burying him, they hung his corpse up on a cross and pelted him with stones.

That was the end of the evil priest. Things were looking up for the congregation, for in his place they appointed a righteous man to be their priest. Salmân ☙ later attested to his piety: "With the exception of those who perform the five prayers (i.e., those from the nation of Muhammad ﷺ), I have never seen anyone who was better, more abstemious when it came to worldly pleasures, more desirous of the Hereafter, or more dedicated to worship throughout the night and day than him. I loved him with a love that I had never known before."

Salmân 🕉 remained with that righteous priest for a while – actually, until the latter died. When the priest was on his deathbed, Salmân 🕉 said, "While I have been here with you, I have loved you with such a love that I have never felt for anyone before you. But, as you know, Allâh's decree is descending upon you now, so whom do you advise me to go to? What do you order me to do?"

"My son, by Allâh, some have perished, others have distorted the teachings of our religion, and yet others have forsaken most of its teachings," said the priest. "I know of no one who is upon that which I am upon except for a man who lives in Al-Musal, so go to him."

After the righteous priest died and was subsequently buried, Salmân 🕉 traveled to Al-Mausil. When he met with the man he was looking for, he said, "O so and so, so and so, upon his deathbed, advised me to come to you. He told me that you are upon the way he followed."

"Stay with me," said this priest. Having then stayed with him for a while, Salmân 🕉 found that he was indeed similar in character to the other righteous priest. But soon these two were also to be parted, for the time of the priest's death was near at hand. When the priest was on his deathbed, Salmân 🕉 said, "Verily, so and so had advised me to come to you and to live with you. Indeed, as you see, Allâh's decree is

descending upon you, so whom do you advise me to go to?
What do you order me to do?"

"My son, by Allâh, I know of no man who is upon that
which we were upon except for a man who lives in Nasibin.
He is so and so, so go to him." When Salmân ؓ met the man
in Nasibin, he told him his story, after which his new
acquaintance told him that he could stay with him. When a
short while passed in the man's company, Salmân ؓ
realized that he was as righteous and good as his two
companions. But soon after Salmân ؓ had made
acquaintance with him, the man was lying on his
deathbed. And again, Salmân ؓ asked him to direct him
to someone else who followed his way. The man directed
him to a priest who lived in the lands of the Romans. When
Salmân ؓ met up with the priest, he told him his story, after
which the priest gave Salmân ؓ permission to stay with
him.

By now, you will not be surprised to learn that this priest too
was righteous and he too was soon lying down on his
deathbed. What was different in the case of this priest is that
he knew no one else that was upon his way. He said, "My
son, by Allâh, I know of no person today who is upon that
which we were upon. Nonetheless, the time draws near
when a Prophet, who is upon the religion of Abraham
(Ibrâhim ﷺ), will come out in the land of the Arabs. And he
will migrate to a land that is bordered on both sides by land
that is replete with volcanic rock (i.e., Al-Madinah); the land
he will migrate to contains date palm trees. He will have
clear, unhidden signs [by which you can recognize him]: he
will eat what is given to him as a gift, but he will not eat
what is given to him as charity. And between his shoulders
is the stamp of prophethood. If you are able to travel to that

land, then do so." After the priest died and was subsequently buried, Salmân ﷺ stayed where he was for a while. While he was with the priest, Salmân ﷺ had managed to earn quite a decent living for himself; he even became the owner of many cows and sheep. When a group of businessmen from the tribe of Kalb passed through the town Salmân ﷺ was living in, Salmân ﷺ said to them, "Take me to the land of the Arabs, and in return for your services, I will give you all of my cows and sheep." Since it was a wonderful and generous offer, they immediately agreed.

Without giving any second thought to the matter, Salmân ﷺ gave them his cows and sheep. At first, the people of the caravan spoke to Salmân ﷺ in a very kind and obsequious manner, but no sooner did they reach Wâdi Al-Qurah than did their true nature become apparent to Salmân ﷺ. They took him to the market and sold him as a slave. This new turn of events did not sadden Salmân ﷺ: true, he had just been sold to a Jewish man as a slave, but his heart was filled with yearning and a strong desire to meet the Prophet whose advent had been prophesied by his priest friend. Salmân ﷺ was actually happy, for he now found himself to be in the city of Yathrib – which later became known as Al-Madinah – a city whose land was in harmony with the description given to him by the priest.

Salmân ﷺ had further cause for joy, for he was able to find out about Muhammad ﷺ and his Companions ﷺ and about how they were about to migrate from Makkah to Yathrib. Though he spent his days toiling in the service of his masters, Salmân ﷺ took advantage of every opportunity he could to find out about the coming of Muhammad ﷺ. When Muhammad ﷺ arrived at Al-Quba, Salmân's Jewish masters and other leaders of the Jewish community in

Yathrib nervously discussed the implications of Muhammad's arrival.

Salmân ؓ learned about his arrival while he was one day working high up in a tree, picking dates for his master. His Master's nephew came running until he stood panting at the foot of a tree beside his uncle. He said, "By Allâh, they are now gathered at Quba, for a man who claims to be a Prophet has come to them from Makkah." After all that Salmân's heart become bright this news was too much for him to take silently. Thrilled with joy, Salmân ؓ descended from the tree and exclaimed, "What are you saying? He has come to Quba? He claims to be a Prophet?" Salmân's master became so angry at his forwardness that he struck him with a severe blow, after which he said, "What does this have to do with you? Go back to your work!"

The joy Salmân ؓ now felt was too much for him to mind being struck so hard by his master. Having planned for this moment for a while now, Salmân ؓ was able to save a number of dates that he had worked hard to earn. He probably had to skip many meals, but that was a welcome sacrifice, since the dates were a necessary part of his plan. At the first opportunity he had, Salmân ؓ went to visit the Messenger of Allâh ﷺ. When he reached him, Salmân ؓ said, "Verily, I have been told that you are indeed a righteous man and that with you are non-native and poor Companions. And this is something I have been saving up for charity. I feel that you are more deserving of this than anyone else." When Salmân ؓ then held out the dates, the Messenger of Allâh ﷺ said to his companions, "Eat," but he abstained from eating any of the dates himself. "This is one (of the signs)," thought Salmân ؓ to himself.

After he returned to his duties, Salmân ؓ began to save

dates again until he had enough to go and make another visit to the Prophet 🙵, who by then had established himself in Al-Madinah. When he went to the Prophet 🙵 with the dates he had saved, he said, "Verily, I noticed that you do not eat what is given in charity, and so this is a gift that I now honor you with." The Messenger of Allâh 🙵 ate from the dates, and he 🙵 ordered his Companions 🙵 to eat from them as well. "That makes two," thought Salmân 🙵 to himself. There remained a third and final proof: the stamp of prophethood. But this was the most difficult to establish, for how was Salmân 🙵 going to be able to steal a glance at the Prophet's back.

Not too long thereafter, Salmân 🙵 went to Messenger of Allâh 🙵, who was in the graveyard of Al-Madinah, following the funeral of Kulthûm bin Al-Hadm 🙵. This seemed to be the perfect opportunity for Salmân 🙵, because if the Prophet 🙵 was going to participate in the digging, perhaps his shirt might be raised high enough so that Salmân 🙵 could see if the stamp of prophethood was there on his back. Wherever the Prophet 🙵 turned, Salmân 🙵 turned with him, so that he constantly stood behind him. The Messenger of Allâh 🙵 noticed what Salmân 🙵 was doing, and so lifting up his shirt, the Prophet 🙵 showed him his back. There clear and plain between the Prophet's shoulders was the stamp that Salmân 🙵 was ardently looking for. Salmân's long and arduous journey for the truth had finally come to an end. Immediately recognizing the Prophet 🙵 for who he really was, Salmân 🙵 hugged him and began to cry.

They both then sat down together, and Salmân 🙵 told the Prophet 🙵 his entire story, from the day he left his hometown until the day he reached Al-Madinah. Without having the least shred of doubt in his mind, Salmân ؓ announced his acceptance of Islam. Just as Bilâl bin Rabâh ؓ was the first person from Al-Ḥabashah to embrace Islam, and Suhaib bin Sinân ؓ was the first Roman to accept Islam – Salmân Al-Fârisi ؓ was the first person from Fâris to embrace Islam.[1]

Salmân's Lineage

Al-Bukhâri reported that Salmân Al-Fârisi's full name was Mâbah bin (son of) Budhakshân bin Mûrsalân bin Bahyudhân bin Fairûzbin Sihrâk child of Āb Al-Malik. It is said that Salmân ؓ was actually from the town of Jai'; however, according to one account, he was from Asbahân.

Whenever Salmân ؓ was asked, "Whose son are you?" he ؓ would answer, "I am Salmân son of Al-Islam, and I am from the children of Adam."[2] Because of his noble character, he became known among the people as, Salmân the Good.

Salmân's Emancipation

When Salmân ؓ found the Messenger of Allâh ﷺ, his journey to seek out the truth had finally come to a successful end. However, there remained one problem: he was still a slave. While the other Companions ؓ were able and free to learn from the Prophet ﷺ and accompany him on military expeditions, Salmân ؓ was busy serving his owners. And so the Messenger of Allâh ﷺ asked his Companions ؓ to help their brother Salmân ؓ. They managed to gather 300 palm

---

[1] *Ahmad* 5/441-444 and others, *Al-Hakim* 3/599 and Albani reported in *Sahih As-Sirah* 70.

[2] Abdur-Razzaq in *Musannaf* 20942.

seedlings for Salmân 🙵; the Prophet ﷺ planted all of them with his noble hand, except for one, which Salmân 🙵 planted. Salmân 🙵 later said, "By the One Who has the soul of Salmân in His Hand, not a single seedling died (i.e., they all grew into date trees), except for the one that Salmân planted." Such was the blessedness of the Messenger of Allâh ﷺ. Also, the Messenger of Allâh ﷺ gave Salmân 🙵 forty measures of gold. With all of this help that he received, Salmân 🙵 was able to purchase his freedom from his Jewish owner.

The First Muslim Engineer

The gathering of the confederate armies for the Battle of Al-Ahzâb represented an unprecedented danger to the Muslims. In previous major battles, the Muslims were pitted against one foe: the Quraish. This time around the Quraish joined forces with other tribes, which is why they become known as the Confederates. They began their march towards Al-Madinah with 10,000 fighters, all under the leadership of Abu Sufyân.

When the Messenger of Allâh ﷺ learned of their plans, he ﷺ consulted his Companions 🙵, asking them whether they thought it best to fight from within Al-Madinah or to go out and face the enemy. No one dared offer any advice in the matter. They still felt remorse for the Day of Uhud, when they had convinced the Prophet ﷺ to go out and face the enemy instead of waiting for them inside of Al-Madinah; and that battle did not go well for the Muslims. They therefore hoped that this time around Allâh ﷺ would send down revelation, guiding the Prophet ﷺ to the best course of action.

While the Companions ☙ sat silently, all confused as to the best course of action, Salmân Al-Fârisi ☙ came forward to offer his opinion in the matter. Since his arrival in Al-Madinah, Salmân ☙ had availed himself of the opportunity of studying Al-Madinah's terrain. And so he knew that from the West and East, Al-Madinah was surrounded by rough terrain that was replete with volcanic rock. It was therefore impossible for the Quraish to launch an attack on Al-Madinah from its eastern or western front. And thick clusters of date-palm trees as well as a mountain bordered Al-Madinah from the south. Therefore, the Quraish and its allies could only attack Al-Madinah from its northern front; hence Salmân's idea.

Salmân ☙ said, "O Messenger of Allâh, in the land of Fâris, when we feared the approach of horses (from an attacking army), we would dig trenches around us (so as to prevent the invading army from entering our cities)."[1] And so Salmân ☙ suggested that the Muslims should dig trenches all along the northern front of Al-Madinah. The Messenger of Allâh ﷺ announced that he agreed with Salmân Al-Fârisi's suggestion and convinced the rest of his Companions ☙ that it was the best course of action that they could take.

"Salmân is from us, the People of (My) Household."

Through the bonds of Islamic brotherhood, Salmân Al-Fârisi ☙ fit in very well among his brothers of faith. And because of his noble character, he became very popular among the Prophet's Companions ☙. Physically, Salmân ☙ was very strong; he did the work of ten men. And he gained the

---

[1] *Ibn Is-haq* 3/235, *Al-Waqidi* 2/445 and *At-Tabari* 1/1465.

admiration of all during the digging of the trenches, when he displayed a prodigious degree of skill and strength. The *Muhâjirûn* and the *Ansâr* began to compete over Salmân ﷺ, who was from neither of the two groups (He wasn't a native dweller of Al-Madinah, and he didn't migrate to Al-Madinah from Makkah). The former group said that Salmân was a Muhâjir – at least an honorary Muhâjir – while the latter group argued that he was an *Ansâri*. The *Muhâjirûn* said, "He is from us." The *Ansâr* said, "He is from us." But the Prophet ﷺ then said,

«سَلْمَانُ مِنَّا أَهْلَ الْبَيْتِ»

"Salmân is from us, the people of [my] household."[1]

This saying of the Prophet ﷺ of course raised Salmân's ranking among the Muslims, which was probably the desired effect that the Prophet ﷺ had in mind. But perhaps the Prophet ﷺ was also alluding to something else: Salmân ﷺ, who was from the people of Fâris, could trace his roots all the way back to Ibrâhim ﷺ, who was a great-grandfather of the Prophet ﷺ. And Allâh ﷻ knows best.

Bonds of Brotherhood

Upon arriving in Al-Madinah, the Prophet ﷺ established bonds of brotherhood between the *Ansâr* and the *Muhâjirûn*. As for Salmân Al-Fârisi ﷺ, the Prophet ﷺ assigned Abu Ad-Dardâ' ﷺ to be his brother.

---

[1] *Al-Waqdi* 2/445 At-Tabrani reported in *Al-Kabir*, see *Al-Majma'* 6/130 and Al-Hakim in *Mustadrak* 3/597.

Salmân's Ranking Among the Muslims

Salmân's ranking among the Muslims took a considerable leap when the Prophet ﷺ accepted his advice to dig trenches in order to prevent the confederate armies from entering Al-Madinah. Allâh ﷻ said:

﴿وَشَاوِرْهُمْ فِى ٱلْأَمْرِ﴾

"And consult them in the affairs"[1]

And Allâh ﷻ said:

﴿وَٱلَّذِينَ ٱسْتَجَابُوا۟ لِرَبِّهِمْ وَأَقَامُوا۟ ٱلصَّلَوٰةَ وَأَمْرُهُمْ شُورَىٰ بَيْنَهُمْ وَمِمَّا رَزَقْنَٰهُمْ يُنفِقُونَ ﴿٣٨﴾﴾

"And those who answer the Call of their Lord [i.e., to believe that He is the only One Lord (Allâh), and to worship none but Him Alone], and perform As-Salat (Iqamat-as-Salat), and who (conduct) their affairs by mutual consultation, and who spend of what We have bestowed on them."[2]

In the end, Salmân's advice paid off, for after a long siege, the confederates were forced, by the will of Allâh ﷻ, to return to their homes. Despite the hugeness of their army, they retreated without having inflicted any serious harm upon the Muslims.

Salmân's ranking also increased by dint of the fact that the Prophet ﷺ praised him on more than one occasion. According to one *Mursal* narration that is related by Al-Hasan, the Prophet ﷺ said:

---

[1] *Qur'ân* 3: 159.
[2] *Qur'ân* 42: 38.

«سَلْمَانُ سَابِقُ فَارِسَ – إِلَى الْإِسْلَامِ»

"Salmân is the first person from the people of Fâris to (embrace) Islam."[1]

In a narration that is related by Abu Hurairah 🙏 in Al-Baihaqi, the Prophet ﷺ said:

«لَوْ كَانَ الْإِيمَانُ عِنْدَ الثُّرَيَّا لَتَنَاوَلَهُ رِجَالٌ مِنْ فَارِسَ»

"Had Eemân (Faith) been found at Ath-Thurayyah (the name given to a constellation of stars), a man from Fâris would have (managed to) obtain it."[2]

In a narration that is found in *Sahih Bukhâri*, the Prophet ﷺ said similar words, while placing his hand on Salmân 🙏. Salmân 🙏 was also known for being learned in both the *Injil* – through his studies with the various priests he learned from – and the Qur'ân. After the Prophet ﷺ died, Salmân 🙏 took part in the conquering of areas that were part of the Fâris Empire. It was a most fitting end, then, that he, who was from the people of Fâris, became *Amir* (Governor) of many cities in that land.

His Death

Salmân 🙏 died in the year 36 H and was buried somewhere in the lands over which he was governor.

---

[1] *Al-Hakim* 3/285
[2] *Al-Bukhari* 4897 and *Muslim* 2546

'Abdullâh bin Rawâhah

'Abdullâh bin Rawâhah ﷺ

His Lineage

He is 'Abdullâh bin (son of) Rawâhah bin Tha'labah bin 'Imra'ul-Qais bin 'Amr bin 'Imra'ul-Qais bin Mâlik bin Al-Aghar bin Tha'labah bin Ka'b bin Al-Khazraj Al-Ansâri. He ﷺ was a famous poet, and by dint of that fact, he became one of the poets of the Prophet ﷺ.

His *Kunyah*

The exact *Kunyah* of 'Abdullâh bin Rawâhah ﷺ is not agreed upon by historians. Some historians say that his *Kunyah* was Abu Muhammad; others say that it was Abu Rawâhah; and yet others say that it was Abu 'Amr.

His Mother

His mother was Kabshah daughter of Wâqid bin 'Amr bin Al-Itnâbah, from the Khazraj tribe.

One of the Leading Delegates During the Second 'Aqabah Pledge

On the night of Al-'Aqabah, the Messenger of Allâh ﷺ asked the *Ansâr* to choose twelve leaders among themselves to represent the rest of them. They chose nine leaders from the Khazraj tribe, and three from the 'Aus tribe. Of the former nine, two were representatives from the Banu Hârith clan: Sa'd bin Ar-Rabi' ﷺ and 'Abdullâh bin Rawâhah. When it was his turn to pledge allegiance, 'Abdullâh bin Rawâhah ﷺ said, "I pledge to you, O Messenger of Allâh, the same pledge that the 12 Naqib (leaders) from the Children of Israel made to 'Īesâ bin Maryam ﷺ."

Bonds of Brotherhood

Shortly after his arrival in Al-Madinah, the Prophet ﷺ established many bonds of brotherhood; one such bond was established between Al-Miqdâd bin 'Amr ﷺ and 'Abdullâh bin Rawâhah ﷺ.

A Messenger of the Messenger of Allâh ﷺ

Just after Allâh ﷺ granted victory to the Messenger of Allâh ﷺ and the Muslims on the Day of Badr, the Messenger of Allâh ﷺ sent Zaid bin Hârithah ﷺ and 'Abdullâh bin Rawâhah ﷺ back to Al-Madinah before the others as bearers of glad tidings. They arrived on the outskirts of Al-Madinah on a Sunday morning. Upon returning, 'Abdullâh bin Rawâhah ﷺ began to call out, "O people of the *Ansâr*, rejoice over the safety of the Messenger of Allâh ﷺ and the death and capture of the polytheists. Ibn Rabi'ah, the two sons of Al-Hajjâj, Abu Jahl, Zam'ah bin Al-Aswad, and Umayyah bin Khalaf — all of these were killed [during the battle]. Furthermore, Suhail bin 'Amr and Dhul-'Anyâb are among the many prisoners."

'Āsim bin 'Adi accosted 'Abdullâh bin Rawâhah ﷺ and said, "Is what you say true, O son of Rawâhah?"

"Yes, by Allâh," answered 'Abdullâh ﷺ. "*In shâ Allâh* (if Allâh wills), the Messenger of Allâh ﷺ is returning, and with him are the prisoners... "

'Abdullâh bin Rawâhah ﷺ then continued walking, stopping at each house to announce the good news. Young children joined him as they called out, "Abu Jahl the evildoer has died!"

The Messenger of Allâh ﷺ Consults 'Abdullâh bin Rawâhah ﷺ

When the Messenger of Allâh ﷺ consulted his Companions ﷺ about the prisoners of Badr, Abu Bakr ﷺ said, "Ransom (them)." Meanwhile 'Umar ﷺ suggested that the prisoners be killed. And 'Abdullâh bin Rawâhah ﷺ agreed with 'Umar ﷺ, though he took even a sterner stance, saying that the prisoners should be burned to death.[1] The Quraish had, after all, ruthlessly persecuted the Muslims for 13 years; and then they had the temerity to steal all of the wealth that the Muslims had left behind in Makkah.

'Abdullâh bin Rawâhah ﷺ, the Poet

Sweet yet powerful words of poetry would issue forth from the mouth of 'Abdullâh bin Rawâhah ﷺ. From the day that he placed his hand in the hand of the Messenger of Allâh ﷺ, pledged allegiance to him, and pronounced the Testimony of Truth, Ibn Rawâhah ﷺ employed his poetic talents for the cause of Islam. He ﷺ, like Hassân bin Thâbit ﷺ and Ka'b bin Mâlik ﷺ, was one of the Prophet's poets.

Allâh ﷺ said:

---

[1] *Ahmad* 1/383. It is weak *Hadith*.

$$\lllll \text{وَٱلشُّعَرَآءُ يَتَّبِعُهُمُ ٱلْغَاوُۥنَ} \,\textcircled{٢٢٤} \rlll$$

"As for the poets, the erring follow them."[1]

When this verse was revealed, 'Abdullâh bin Rawâhah ﷺ said, "Indeed, Allâh knows that I am one of them." Then Allâh ﷻ revealed the following verse:

$$\lllll \text{إِلَّا ٱلَّذِينَ ءَامَنُوا۟ وَعَمِلُوا۟ ٱلصَّٰلِحَٰتِ وَذَكَرُوا۟ ٱللَّهَ كَثِيرًا وَٱنتَصَرُوا۟ مِنۢ بَعْدِ مَا}$$
$$\text{ظُلِمُوا۟ وَسَيَعْلَمُ ٱلَّذِينَ ظَلَمُوٓا۟ أَىَّ مُنقَلَبٍ يَنقَلِبُونَ} \,\textcircled{٢٢٧} \rlll$$

"Except those who believe (in the Oneness of Allâh – Islamic Monotheism), and do righteous deeds, and remember Allâh much, and reply back (in poetry) to the unjust poetry (which the pagan poets utter against the Muslims). And those who do wrong will come to know by what overturning they will be overturned."[2]

It was only when this Verse was revealed that 'Abdullâh bin Rawâhah ﷺ felt at ease again.

'Abdullâh bin Rawâhah's Feats on the Battlefield

While he was alive, 'Abdullâh bin Rawâhah ﷺ took part in all of the major battles that took place between the Muslims and the polytheists: Badr, Uhud, Ahzâb, Al-Hudaibiyyah, and Khaibar.

One year after the Treaty of Hudaibiyyah was ratified, the Messenger of Allâh ﷺ returned to Makkah, along with 1000 Muslims, in order to perform *'Umrah*. For the duration of the Prophet's stay in Makkah, the polytheists retreated to the hilltops of Makkah. While the Messenger of Allâh ﷺ was

---

[1] *Qur'ân* 26: 224.
[2] *Qur'ân* 26: 227.

making circuits around the Ka'bah, and while the Quraish were observing him and the Muslims from their perched positions, 'Abdullâh bin Rawâhah 🕮 walked in front of the Messenger of Allâh 🕮 and recited Verses of poetry. Guidance from Allâh, giving charity, prayer, and the transgressions of the Quraish (not mentioning them by name but alluding to them) – these were the themes of the poem that 'Abdullâh bin Rawâhah 🕮 was reciting.

'Umar bin Al-Khattâb 🕮, who was in close proximity to the Messenger of Allâh 🕮, became angry and said, "O Ibn Rawâhah, do you speak this poetry in the Haram (Inviolable place) of Allâh and in the presence of the Messenger of Allâh 🕮?"

"Leave him, O 'Umar," said the Messenger of Allâh 🕮.

«خَلِّ عَنْهُ يَا عُمَرُ، فَوَ الَّذِي نَفْسِي بِيَدِهِ لَكَلَامُهُ أَشَدُّ عَلَيْهِمْ – الكفار أو المشركين– مِنْ وَقْعِ النَّبْلِ»

"For by the One Who has my soul in His Hand, his ('Abdullâh's) speech is more severe upon them (upon the Quraish, who were listening and watching the Muslims from a distance) than (them) being struck by arrows."[1]

Anas bin Mâlik 🕮, the servant of the Messenger of Allâh 🕮 said, "When 'Abdullâh bin Rawâhah would meet one of his companions, he would say to him, 'Come and let us believe in our Lord for an hour (i.e., let us sit together to remember, praise, and glorify our Lord)." And according to another narration, the Prophet 🕮 said:

«نِعْمَ الرَّجُلُ عَبْدُاللهِ بْنُ رَوَاحَةَ»

---

[1] *At-Tirmidhi* 2847.

"Abdullâh bin Rawâhah is indeed a good (honorable, blessed) man."[1]

The Day of Mo'tah

In the year 7 H, the Messenger of Allâh ﷺ sent letters to the kings and leaders of foreign lands, inviting them to embrace Islam. Among those who carried those letters was Al-Hârith bin 'Umair Al-Azdi ﷺ, whose task it was to go to the king of Busra Ash-Sham. When Al-Hârith ﷺ stopped at Mo'tah, he was confronted by Shurahbil bin 'Amr Al-Ghassâni, one of Caesar's governors over Ash-Sham. Shurahbil killed the messenger ﷺ of the Messenger of Allâh ﷺ, and so the purpose of the Mo'tah expedition was to teach Shurahbil Al-Ghassâni a lesson. For this expedition, the Prophet ﷺ assembled an army that consisted of 3000 fighters.

The Prophet ﷺ escorted the army until they were about 3 miles outside of Al-Madinah. It was then that the Prophet ﷺ appointed a leader over the army. He ﷺ said:

«زَيْدُ بْنُ حَارِثَةَ أَمِيرٌ عَلَى النَّاسِ، فَإِنْ قُتِلَ زَيْدٌ فَجَعْفَرُ بْنُ أَبِي طَالِبٍ، فَإِنْ قُتِلَ جَعْفَرٌ فَعَبْدُاللهِ بْنُ رَوَاحَةَ، فَإِنْ قُتِلَ عَبْدُاللهِ بْنُ رَوَاحَةَ فَلْيَرْتَضِ الْمُسْلِمُونَ بَيْنَهُمْ رَجُلًا فَلْيَجْعَلُوهُ عَلَيْهِمْ»

"Zaid bin Hârithah is the leader over the people (i.e., over the army). If he is killed, then Ja'far bin Abi Tâlib will take his place (as leader). And if he is killed, then 'Abdullâh bin Rawâhah will take his place (as leader). And if 'Abdullâh bin Rawâhah is killed, then let the Muslims be pleased with a man among them and appoint him to be their

---

[1] Reported by Ibn Asakir 30/67.

leader.''[1]

When the army reached its destination, they found that the Romans had prepared for their coming a huge army, one that consisted of more than 200,000 fighters. Because the Muslims were outnumbered by at least 66 to 1, some of the Muslims thought it best to send news back to the Prophet ﷺ and wait for reinforcements to arrive. 'Abdullâh bin Rawâhah ﷺ had an entirely different view in the matter; he felt that it was best to continue on their mission, regardless of the outcome. And so he delivered a heartfelt speech to the Muslim soldiers: "O people, by Allâh, what you are disliking [now] is the very thing that you had come for in the first place: You came seeking martyrdom. And we do not fight people with numbers or strength. We do not fight them except with this religion, which Allâh ﷺ has honored us with. Therefore, it is only one of two good endings: Either victory or martyrdom."

"By Allâh, Ibn Rawâhah has spoken the truth," was the resounding response of the soldiers, and so they proceeded forth to do battle.

The Prophet's instructions represented a kind of prophecy concerning the impending battle, and, of course, it proved true. For when the armies met in combat, Zaid bin Hârithah ﷺ was killed. Taking the banner of the Messenger of Allâh ﷺ in his hand, Ja'far bin Abi Tâlib ﷺ took over as the leader of the army, but he too was soon killed. Then 'Abdullâh bin Rawâhah ﷺ took the banner and continued to fight until he too was killed.

---

[1] *Al-Musnad* 1/204 and see *Al-Fathul-Bari* 4261, and last part in *Usdul-Gabah* 3/237.

Back in Al-Madinah

Meanwhile, back in Al-Madinah, the Messenger of Allâh ﷺ
called out for the people to gather. When the people had
made their way to the *Masjid*, the Prophet ﷺ, with tears
flowing from his eyes, ascended the pulpit. He ﷺ then said:

«أَيُّهَا النَّاسُ نَابَ خَبَرٌ أَوْ ثَابَ بَابُ خَيْرٍ، أُخْبِرُكُمْ عَنْ جِيْشِكُمْ هَذَا
الْغَازِي، إِنَّهُمُ انْطَلَقُوا فَلَقُوا الْعَدُوَّ، فَقُتِلَ زَيْدٌ رَضِيَ اللهُ تَعَالَى عَنْهُ
شَهِيدًا، فَاسْتَغْفِرُوا لَهُ، ثُمَّ أَخَذَ الرَّايَةَ جَعْفَرٌ رَضِيَ اللهُ عَنْهُ فَشَدَّ عَلَى
الْقَوْمِ حَتَّى قُتِلَ شَهِيدًا، فَاسْتَغْفِرُوا لَهُ، ثُمَّ أَخَذَ الرَّايَةَ عَبْدُاللهِ بْنُ
رَوَاحَةَ رَضِيَ اللهُ عَنْهُ وَأَثْبَتَ قَدَمَيْهِ حَتَّى قُتِلَ شَهِيدًا فَاسْتَغْفِرُوا لَهُ،
ثُمَّ أَخَذَ اللِّوَاءَ خَالِدُ بْنُ الْوَلِيدِ وَلَمْ يَكُنْ مِنَ الْأُمَرَاءِ وَهُوَ أَمِيرُ نَفْسِهِ،
وَلَكِنَّهُ سَيْفٌ مِنْ سُيُوفِ اللهِ فَآبَ ‪-‬ رجع ‪-‬ بِنَصْرِهِ.»

*"O people, a door of goodness, a door of goodness, a door
of goodness. I will inform you about your army that has
set out for battle. They proceeded forward and met with
the enemy. Zaid, may Allâh be pleased with him, was
killed a martyr, so ask forgiveness for him. Then Ja'far,
may Allâh be pleased with him, took the banner. He
fought strongly against the people (i.e., the enemy), until
he was killed a martyr, so ask forgiveness for him. Then
'Abdullâh bin Rawâhah, may Allâh be pleased with him,
took the banner. He planted his feet firmly [on the
battlefield (and fought bravely)] until he was killed a
martyr, so ask forgiveness for him. Then Khâlid bin Al-
Walid, who was not from the (appointed) leaders, took up
the flag. And he is the leader of his own self, but he is a
sword from the swords of Allâh, and so he then returned*

with His (Allâh's) help (i.e., the army then retreated from the battlefield under the leadership of Khâlid , and were returning safely to Al-Madinah; by the permission of Allâh, the Prophet was able to see all of these events while he himself was in Al-Madinah)."[1]

Words of Praise for 'Abdullâh bin Rawâhah

The Messenger of Allâh said:

«رَحِمَ اللهُ ابْنَ رَوَاحَةَ إِنَّهُ يُحِبُّ الْمَجَالِسَ الَّتِي تَتَبَاهَى بِهَا الْمَلَائِكَةُ»

"May Allâh have mercy on Ibn Rawâhah. He indeed loves those gatherings that are displayed to the angels (i.e., gatherings wherein Allâh is remembered)."[2]

When a man later married the widow of 'Abdullâh bin Rawâhah , he asked her to tell him about some noteworthy deed that 'Abdullâh used to perform. She said, "Whenever he intended to leave his house, he would perform two units of prayer. And whenever he would enter his house, he would perform two units of prayer. This is a practice that he never abandoned."[3]

---

[1] *Ahmad* 5/299 and At-Tabari in his book *Tarikh* 3/41.
[2] *Ahmad* 3/265.
[3] *Usdul-Gabah* 3/336.

Al-Hubâb bin Al-Mundhir رضي الله عنه

Al-Hubâb bin Al-Mundhir

His Lineage

He is Al-Hubâb bin Al-Mundhir bin Al-Jamûh bin Zaid bin Harâm bin Ka'ab bin 'Atam bin Ka'b bin Salamah Al-Ansâri, Al-Khazraji, and then As-Sulami.

His *Kunyah*

His *Kunyah* is Abu 'Amr.

The Day of Badr

When the Prophet ﷺ set out with about 300 Muslims to overtake Abu Sufyân's trading caravan, news of their approach reached Abu Sufyân, who then, with a great deal of skill and cunning, was able to change his course and flee from the oncoming Muslims. At the same time, he had managed to send news to the Quraish about his predicament. And so headed mainly by Abu Jahl, the Quraish set out with the intention of not only saving their caravan, but also destroying the Muslims before they would have the opportunity of becoming stronger and increasing in numbers. What resulted from these events was the Battle of Badr, which took place two years after the Prophet ﷺ migrated to Al-Madinah. Before the commencement of this battle, the Prophet ﷺ handed the banner of the Khazraj tribe to Al-Hubâb bin Al-Mundhir ﷺ.

The Wise Counsel of Al-Hubâb bin Al-Mundhir ﷺ

With Abu Sufyân's caravan out of the picture and a serious military engagement inevitable, the situation soon precipitated into a race to the wells of Badr; for if the battle were going to be drawn out, the army that had control of the water supply would certainly have the upper hand. The Prophet ﷺ and the Muslims arrived at the wells first, and when they stopped to make camp, Al-Hubâb bin Al-Mundhir ﷺ said, "O Messenger of Allâh, was this spot revealed from Allâh ﷻ, so that it is not right for us to move ahead of it or behind it? Or is this (the decision to make camp here) based on opinion, warfare, and strategy?" The Prophet ﷺ confirmed that it was based on opinion and the strategy of warfare. Had the decision to make camp where they had stopped been based on revelation, Al-Hubâb ﷺ would not have uttered another word. But being that that was not the case, being that the Prophet ﷺ encouraged the counsels of his Companions, and being that Al-Hubâb ﷺ knew that it was his duty to give good and sincere advice, Al-Hubâb ﷺ suggested another course of action.

﴿فَبِمَا رَحْمَةٍ مِّنَ اللَّهِ لِنتَ لَهُمْ وَلَوْ كُنتَ فَظًّا غَلِيظَ ٱلْقَلْبِ لَٱنفَضُّوا۟ مِنْ حَوْلِكَ فَٱعْفُ عَنْهُمْ وَٱسْتَغْفِرْ لَهُمْ وَشَاوِرْهُمْ فِى ٱلْأَمْرِ فَإِذَا عَزَمْتَ فَتَوَكَّلْ عَلَى ٱللَّهِ إِنَّ ٱللَّهَ يُحِبُّ ٱلْمُتَوَكِّلِينَ ۝﴾

"And by the Mercy of Allâh, you dealt with them gently. And had you been severe and harsh-hearted, they would have broken away from about you; so pass over (their faults), and ask (Allâh's) Forgiveness for them; and

consult them in the affairs. Then when you have taken a decision, put your trust in Allâh, certainly, Allâh loves those who put their trust (in Him)."[1]

Al-Hubâb 🙞 said, "O Messenger of Allâh, this is not a good spot (to make camp). Lead the people until we reach the well that is closest to the people (the enemy), for I indeed know that it contains plentiful water... " He continued to say that the Muslims should build a reservoir over the well and destroy all of the other wells; this way, Al-Hubâb 🙞 said, "We will drink, and they will not drink." The Prophet 🙵 agreed to implement Al-Hubâb's plan; in fact, according to one narration, Ibn 'Abbâs 🙞 said, "Jibril 🙲 descended to the Messenger of Allâh 🙵 and said, 'The correct view is the one that Al-Hubâb bin Al-Mundhir suggested.'" Based on the orders of the Prophet 🙵, Al-Hubâb's plan was then implemented.

Al-Hubâb bin Al-Mundhir 🙞 participated in the next major battle as well: The Battle of Uhud. When many of the Muslims began to flee, Al-Hubâb bin Al-Mundhir 🙞 was one of the few who remained firm alongside the Messenger of Allâh 🙵, pledging to remain firm beside him 🙵 until the very end.

Banu An-Nadir and Banu Quraizah

When the Banu An-Nadir and Banu Quraizah tribes blatantly violated the terms of the peace treaties that they had made with the Muslims, the Prophet 🙵 consulted with his Companions 🙞. For a second time, Al-Hubâb bin Al-Mundhir 🙞 availed of the opportunity to give wise counsel

---

[1] *Qur'ân* 3: 159.

to the Prophet ﷺ. He ﷺ suggested that the Muslims set camp between the castles of the enemy, so as to prevent them from communicating with one another. And again, the Prophet ﷺ agreed to implement Al-Hubâb's plan.

The Day of Khaibar

The Jews of Khaibar contacted the people of the Ghatafân tribe, who were known to be mercenaries for hire. As a reward for fighting the Muslims, the Jews of Khaibar offered them a percentage of their yearly harvest, which consisted mainly of fruits and dates. They furthermore established alliances with the tribes of Fadak, Taimâ, and Wâdi Al-Qura; together, they were preparing to launch a surprise attack on Al-Madinah. Having been informed of their plans, the Muslims who witnessed Al-Hudaibiyyah traveled to Khaibar, in order to bring an end to the plotting of its inhabitants and their allies.

Khaibar consisted of many fortresses, one of which was called An-Natât. When the Prophet ﷺ arrived at Khaibar, he made camp near the An-Natât fortress. Al-Hubâb bin Al-Mundhir ﷺ approached the Prophet ﷺ and said, "O Messenger of Allâh, as for your decision to make camp here, if it something that you are commanding us to do, then we will not speak (i.e., we will not object). But if it is a matter of opinion (i.e., not a religious ruling from you, but rather a worldly decision that is open to discussion), then we will speak."

"It is a matter of opinion," answered the Prophet ﷺ.

"O Messenger of Allâh," said Al-Hubâb ﷺ, "I have some knowledge about the people of An-Natât. I know of no people who can shoot arrows farther and more accurately than they can. On top of that, they are high above us, so since they are shooting down at us, their arrows will come down (upon us) even faster. And we are not safe (here) from them coming down (upon us with a surprise attack) and entering into the thick cluster of date-trees."

"You have pointed out the best view (in the matter)," said the Prophet ﷺ.

$$ «أَشَرْتَ بِالرَّأْيِ، إِذَا أَمْسَيْنَا إِنْ شَاءَ اللهُ تَحَوَّلْنَا» $$

"In the evening, we will move (to another spot), if Allâh wills."[1]

He ﷺ then summoned Muhammad bin Maslamah ﷺ and said to him, "Search out for a spot that is far off for our camp." Muhammad bin Maslamah ﷺ went out to study the terrain, and upon returning, he ﷺ said, "O Messenger of Allâh, I have found for you a (suitable) place to make camp."

"(Proceed) upon the blessing(s) of Allâh," said the Prophet ﷺ. Accordingly, at nightfall the Muslims moved to the new location, which was at a safe distance from the An-Natât fortress.

Al-Hubâb's Death

Al-Hubâb bin Al-Mundhir ﷺ died during the caliphate of the Leader of the Believers, 'Umar bin Al-Khattâb ﷺ.

---

[1] *Al-Waqidi* 2/643 and *As-Sirah* 2/620.

Usaid bin Hudair ﷺ

Usaid bin Hudair ﷺ

His Lineage:

He is Usaid bin Al-Hudair bin Simâk bin 'Atik bin Imrau'l-Qais bin Zaid bin 'Abdul-Ashhal Al-Ansâri Al-Ashhali. His father was Hudair, the skilled horseman and revered chief of the Aus tribe. He led the Aus in the Bu'âth War, which was the final war that was waged between the Aus and Khazraj tribes – it took place not long before the Prophet's migration to Al-Madinah.

His *Kunyah*

His *Kunyah* was Abu Yahya; however, some reports indicate that his *Kunyah* was Abu 'Atik.

His Islam

Before migrating himself, the Messenger of Allâh ﷺ sent Mus'ab bin 'Umair ﷺ to Al-Madinah in order to invite its non-Muslim inhabitants to Islam and to teach its Muslim inhabitants about their religion. Usaid bin Hudair ﷺ was one among many who accepted Islam at the hands of Mus'ab ﷺ.

The Representative of Banu 'Abdul-Ashhal

Usaid ؇ was one of the delegates that met with the Prophet
ﷺ in a meeting that led to the Second 'Aqabah Pledge;
moreover, when it came to making the pledge, he was one of
the twelve leaders who were chosen to represent the other
delegates. In particular, he was the representative of the
Banu Al-Ashhal clan.[1]

Bonds of Brotherhood

When the Prophet ﷺ established bonds of brotherhood
between the *Muhâjirûn* and the *Ansâr*, he ﷺ assigned to each
member of the *Muhâjirûn* a brother from *Ansâr*. As for Usaid
bin Hudair ؇, his assigned brother was Zaid bin Hârithah
؇.

The Day of Uhud

The Day of Uhud was a difficult day for the Muslims, for it
was a day in which they suffered many losses. When the
Muslims began to lose the upper hand that they had initially
enjoyed during the battle, and when defeat seemed
imminent, many of the Muslims began to flee. Usaid bin
Hudair ؇ was one of the few who remained firm. Showing
both bravery and fighting prowess, he untiringly defended
the Prophet ﷺ from oncoming attackers. During the course
of the battle, he was inflicted with a total of 7 wounds.

The Battle of Banu Al-Mustaliq

Usaid bin Hudair ؇ was known as much for his strong faith

---

[1] At-Tabarani in *Al-Mu'jamul-Kabir* 19/90 and *Ahmad* 3/461 .

as for his forbearance, deliberation, and wisdom. Because of these and other noble qualities, the Messenger of Allâh ﷺ would consult with him in important matters.

As the Muslims were returning from the Battle of Banu Al-Mustaliq, a man named Jahjâh got into a heated argument with Sinân bin Farwah; the former was hired by 'Umar bin Al-Khattâb ﷺ to steer his horse, while the latter was an ally of the Khazraj tribe. The argument quickly precipitated into a brief scuffle, in which Jahjâh struck his opponent, causing blood to flow from Sinân's body. Sinân let out a call for help from his allies: "Come, O people of Khazraj!"

Jahjah made a similar call to his own people: "O group of *Muhâjirûn*! Come, O people of Kinânah! Come, O people of Quraish!" A serious altercation would probably have ensued, had not the Prophet ﷺ intervened. "What is the matter (with you that you) call out the call of ignorance!" Such calls for help from one's fellow tribesman were common during the days of ignorance – pre-Islamic times; however, now that they were all united by Islam, such calls negated the brotherly bonds that existed between them.

The Prophet ﷺ was then informed about the situation – that a man from the *Muhâjirûn* struck a man from the *Ansâr*. The Prophet ﷺ again warned them not to call out for help from their fellow tribesmen against other Muslims. He ﷺ said:

«– دَعُوهَا– أَي تِلْكَ الْكَلِمَةُ الَّتِي هِيَ بِالْفُلَانِ– فَإِنَّهَا مُنْتِنَةٌ – أَي مَذْمُومَةٌ لأَنَّهَا مِنْ دَعْوَى الْجَاهِلِيَّةِ»

"Whoever calls out with the call of ignorance will be included among the things that are thrown into the Hellfire."

"O Messenger of Allâh, even if he (the one guilty of the said offence) fasts and prays and claims that he is a Muslim?" asked those who were present.

«وَإِنْ صَامَ وَإِنْ صَلَّى وَزَعَمَ أَنَّهُ مُسْلِمٌ»

"Even if he fasts and prays and claims that he is a Muslim,"

said the Prophet ﷺ. The matter was thus quickly resolved, and further bloodshed was avoided. However, one man was not satisfied with the way things turned out; he didn't want peace among the Muslims, though he claimed to be one himself. Yes, I am referring to the leader of the hypocrites, 'Abdullâh bin Ubai bin Salûl.

'Abdullâh bin Ubai said to those who were around him, "By Allâh, I have never witnessed a more humiliating day than today. Did they really do this? They (the *Muhâjirûn*) outnumber us in our own land. By Allâh, I thought that I would die before I heard a caller calling out with what I heard. Lo! By Allâh, if we get back to Al-Madinah, the honorable ones among us (referring to himself and the native dwellers of Al-Madinah) will expel the ignoble ones (here, he was referring to the Prophet ﷺ in particular, and the *Muhâjirûn* in general)." Addressing the *Ansâr*, he said, "You have done this to your own selves. You have allowed them into your lands, and you have shared with them your wealth. Lo! By Allâh, were you to stop giving them what you have in your hands (i.e., your wealth), they would go to another land, so stop spending on them... "

When Zaid bin Arqam ؓ heard these words, he ؓ hurried to the Messenger of Allâh ﷺ to tell him what 'Abdullâh bin Ubai had said. "O young boy, perhaps you became angry with him," said the Prophet ﷺ.

"By Allâh, O Messenger of Allâh, I heard him say that," said Zaid ٢.

«لَعَلَّهُ أَخْطَأَ سَمْعُكَ»

"Perhaps you misheard him,"

said the Prophet ٢. Though Zaid ٢ spoke the truth, some people from 'Abdullâh bin Ubai's tribe accused him of lying. One person believed Zaid ٢ for sure: 'Umar bin Al-Khattâb ٢. 'Umar ٢ became so angry that he said, "O Messenger of Allâh, grant me permission to strike the neck of Ibn Ubai."

"How will it be, then," began the Messenger of Allâh ٢:

«إِذَا تَحَدَّثَ النَّاسُ بِأَنَّ مُحَمَّدًا يَقْتُلُ أَصْحَابَهُ»

"when the people begin to say that Muhammad kills his companions."

To avoid any further buildup of tensions, the Messenger of Allâh ٢ immediately ordered the Muslims to continue on their homeward journey. It was midday, which was not a normal time for the Prophet ٢ to continue a journey, which is why Usaid bin Hudair ٢ hurried to the Prophet ٢ and said, "Peace be upon you, as well as the mercy and blessings of Allâh, O Messenger of Allâh. You have set out during an early hour, an hour during which you do not [normally] set out."

Usaid ٢ was then informed about the tensions that were brewing and about what 'Abdullâh bin Ubai had said:

"Then, by Allâh, you are the one who will expel him from Al-Madinah, if Allâh wills," said Usaid. "For he, by Allâh, is the ignoble one and you are the honorable one." But like the Messenger of Allâh ٢, Usaid ٢ wanted to avoid internal strife at all costs. He ٢ began to explain the reasons behind

'Abdullâh bin Ubai's deceptive ways, about how, before the advent of Islam, he was poised to be crowned king of Al-Madinah (then known as Yathrib). "And so he feels that Islam has stripped him of his kingdom," said Usaid. As we can see exemplified in this situation, Usaid ؓ always had a slow, peaceful, balanced, and wise approach to dealing with problems.[1]

His Ranking Among the Muslims

It has been related that the Messenger of Allâh ﷺ said:

«نِعْمَ الرَّجُلُ أُسَيْدُ بْنُ حُضَيْرٍ»

"Usaid bin Hudair is a good (honorable, blessed) man."[2]

And the Mother of the Believers, 'Aishah ؓ, said, "None of three men from the *Ansâr* could be vied with in his overall virtues, and all of them are from (the clan of) Banu 'Abdul-Ashhal: Sa'd bin Mu'âdh, Usaid bin Hudair, and 'Abbâd bin Bishr."

It is true that there are other Companions ؓ, such as Ubai bin Ka'b ؓ and 'Abdullâh bin Mas'ûd ؓ, who were known for their beautiful recitation of the Qur'ân. But although he was less known in this regard, Usaid bin Hudair ؓ also recited the Qur'ân in a beautiful voice. One night, he was reciting the Qur'ân, while his son Yahya ؓ, who was a young boy at the time, was lying down beside him, and nearby his horse was tied up. As Usaid ؓ was reciting the Qur'ân, his horse suddenly became excited. Usaid ؓ stood

---

[1] *Ibn Hisham* 3/303, 304, *Al-Bukhari* 4907 and *At-Tirmidhi* 3313.
[2] *Ahmad* 2/419, *Al-Hakim* 3/289 and *At-Tirmidhi* 3795.

up, feeling alarmed and having no concern except for the safety of his son. Everything seemed to be okay, so he resumed his recitation of the Qur'ân, but again his horse began to move wildly about. Usaid ﷺ stood up for a second time, and for a second time his mind was preoccupied with the safety of his son. The horse calmed down, and Usaid ﷺ resumed his recitation of the Qur'ân. And then for a third time, the horse moved wildly about. This time around, Usaid ﷺ looked up; above him, he saw something that was in the shape of a cloud (or something that gives shade), (and in it) were the likes of lamps, coming down from the sky. This scene terrified Usaid ﷺ, and so he remained silent (until the morning).

When Usaid ﷺ woke up, he went to the Messenger of Allâh ﷺ and informed him about what had happened to him. The Prophet ﷺ said:

«اقْرَأْ أَبَا يَحْيَى»

"Recite, O Abu Yahyah."

"I indeed recited, and my horse became excited and moved about wildly; then I stood up, having no concern except for (the safety of) my son."

"Recite, O Abu Yahya," said the Prophet ﷺ.

"I indeed recited, and my horse became excited and moved about wildly. I indeed recited and then raised my head. There was something (above me) that was in the shape of a cloud (or anything that gives shade), and in it were the likes of lamps, which terrified me."

«تِلْكَ الْمَلَائِكَةُ دَنَوْا لِصَوْتِكَ وَلَوْ قَرَأْتَ حَتَّى تُصْبِحَ لَأَصْبَحَ النَّاسُ يَنْظُرُونَ إِلَيْهِمْ»

"Those were the angels," said the Prophet ﷺ. *"They came near [to you] because of your voice. And had you continued to recite until the morning, people would have been able to see them."*[1]

One dark night, Usaid bin Hudair ؓ and 'Abbâd bin Bishr ؓ went to the house of the Messenger of Allâh ﷺ. Each of the two guests was leaning on a stick. The Messenger of Allâh ﷺ welcomed them, after which they entered into a discussion with him. When the two of them left his house, Usaid bin Hudair's stick lighted up and illuminated the way for him until he returned safely to his house.[2]

After the Prophet ﷺ died, Usaid ؓ continued to strive untiringly for the cause of Islam. Usaid ؓ was a part of the army that, led by 'Umar bin Al-Khattâb ؓ, headed towards Sham (Syria and surrounding regions, such as Palestine) and ended up conquering Jerusalem.

His Death

Usaid bin Hudair ؓ lived a fruitful life, one that was characterized by constant worship and noble sacrifices for the cause of Islam. He ؓ died during the caliphate of 'Umar bin Al-Khattâb ؓ, in the month of Sha'bân, the year 20 H. 'Umar ؓ insisted upon carrying his bier over his shoulders, and it was 'Umar ؓ who led his Funeral prayer. Under the dirt of the Al-Baqi' graveyard, the Companions ؓ buried the body of the noble Companion Usaid bin Hudair ؓ.

---

[1] *Usdul-Ghabah* 241, and *Muslim* 796 and *Ahmad* 3/81.
[2] *Al-Bukhari* 3805.

Usâmah bin Zaid ﷺ

Usâmah bin Zaid ﷺ

His Lineage

He is Usâmah bin Zaid bin Hârithah bin Shurahbil bin Ka'b bin 'Abdul-'Uzza bin Zaid bin Imraul-Qais bin 'Āmir bin An-No'mân bin 'Āmir bin 'Abd Wadd bin Wabrah bin Al-Kalbi. His mother is Umm Aiman ﷺ, the nursemaid of the Prophet ﷺ.

His *Kunyah*

Various historical accounts give conflicting reports about Usâmah's *Kunyah*; here are the different *Kunyah*s that are related in those accounts: Abu Muhammad, Abu Zaid, Abu Yazid, and Abu Khârijah.

A Brief Description

Usâmah bin Zaid ﷺ was black-skinned, with a flat and not raised nose. He had a large stomach, and was correspondingly given the nickname, 'The One with a Stomach.' That he had a large stomach did not in the least have a negative impact upon him, for a man's worth is judged by his religion, his manners, his righteousness, and his beliefs, and not by his outward appearance.

The Prophet's Love for Usâmah ﷺ

The Prophet ﷺ loved Usâmah ﷺ a great deal. 'Abdullâh bin 'Umar ﷺ reported that the Messenger of Allâh ﷺ said:

«إِنَّ أُسَامَةَ بْنَ زَيْدٍ لَأَحَبُّ النَّاسِ إِلَيَّ أَوْ مِنْ أَحَبِّ النَّاسِ إِلَيَّ وَأَنَا أَرْجُو أَنْ يَكُونَ مِنْ صَالِحِيكُمْ فَاسْتَوْصُوا بِهِ خَيْرًا»

"Indeed, Usâmah bin Zaid is the most beloved of people to me, or among the most beloved of people to me. And I indeed hope that he joins the ranks of the righteous ones among you, so treat him well."[1]

Usâmah ﷺ was born after the Prophet ﷺ received revelation for the first time. When Usâmah ﷺ was a child, the Prophet ﷺ would look after him ﷺ; he ﷺ would wipe off nasal mucus from Usâmah's face and clean his nose for him. And he ﷺ said:

«لَوْ كَانَ أُسَامَةُ جَارِيَةً لَزَيَّنَّاهُ وَجَهَّزْنَاهُ وَحَبَّبْنَاهُ إِلَى الْأَزْوَاجِ»

"Had Usâmah been a young girl, we would have adorned him, prepared him [to look good], and made him beloved to husbands (i.e., prospective suitors)."[2]

Riding Behind the Messenger of Allâh ﷺ

One day, shortly after he migrated to Al-Madinah, the Prophet ﷺ sat down on a donkey upon which was a saddle made of coarse material from Fadak (Fadak is the name of a place that is situated near Al-Madinah). And behind him sat Usâmah ﷺ. They were riding towards the homes of the

---

[1] *Usdul-Ghabah* 1/194, *Ahmad* 2/96, *Ibn Sa'd* 4/49 and see *Al-Bukhari* 3730.
[2] Al-Qurtubi in his *Tafsir* 14/239.

Banu Al-Hârith clan, with the intention of visiting Sa'd bin 'Ubâdah ﷺ. However, on their way, they passed by a gathering that contained a mix of Muslims, polytheists, and Jews. 'Abdullâh bin Ubai bin Salûl was among them, and at that time, he had not yet outwardly embraced Islam; I say 'outwardly' because, as is well-known, he did not inwardly embrace Islam, for he was a hypocrite. 'Abdullâh bin Rawâhah ﷺ was also among the attendees of that gathering.

When the loud voice of the donkey could be heard by the attendees of the gathering, 'Abdullâh bin Ubai covered his nose with his robe and said, "Do not raise dust upon us."

The Messenger of Allâh ﷺ of course did not dignify Ibn Ubai's remark with a response; instead, he ﷺ extended greetings of peace, for there were Muslims present in the gathering. The Prophet ﷺ then descended and began to invite them unto Allâh ﷺ and to recite Verses of the Qur'ân to them.

'Abdullâh bin Ubai bin Salûl said, "O person, there is nothing better than what you say, if it is the truth, so do not harm us with it (your speech) in our gatherings. Return to your dwellings. When someone from us comes to you, then relate your stories to him."

'Abdullâh bin Rawâhah ﷺ then spoke up: "Yes, O Messenger of Allâh, enter upon our gatherings, for we do indeed love for you to do so." The Muslims, polytheists, and Jews began to curse one another until they were on the verge of physical combat. The Messenger of Allâh ﷺ continued to make peace between them until they finally calmed down.

The Messenger of Allâh ﷺ then climbed his mount and continued on his previous course until he reached Sa'd's house. Upon entering Sa'd's home, the Prophet ﷺ said:

«يَا سَعْدُ أَلَمْ تَسْمَعْ إِلَى مَا قَالَ أَبُو حُبَابٍ - يَرِيدُ عَبْدَاللهِ بْنَ أُبَيِّ -
قَالَ كَذَا وَكَذَا وَكَذَا»

*"O Sa'd, have you not heard what Abu Hubâb (i.e.,
'Abdullâh bin Ubai) said: (he said) such and such
things."*[1]

"Yes, O Messenger of Allâh, may my father and mother be
held ransom for you," said Sa'd bin 'Ubâdah ﷺ. "Forgive
him and pardon him. For by the One Who has sent down
upon you the Book (the Qur'ân) with the truth, Allâh
brought to you the truth that He revealed to you at a time
when the people of Al-Buhairah (i.e., Al-Madinah) agreed to
crown him (Ibn Ubai) as king [of Yathrib (i.e., Al-Madinah)].
When Allâh prevented that from happening with the truth
that He gave to you, Ibn Ubai was filled with hatred for
what happened. That explains what you saw him do." And
so the Messenger of Allâh ﷺ forgave him.

"Did you kill him even though he said, 'None has the right
to be worshipped but Allâh'"

Once, when the Muslims were engaged in battle with the
polytheists, Usâmah bin Zaid ﷺ had the upper hand against
a man and was about to deliver a lethal blow with his
sword, but the man suddenly said, *"Lâ ilaha illallâh* (None
has the right to be worshipped but Allâh)." Usâmah ﷺ then
finished what he had set out to do, killing the man with one
thrust of his sword. The matter did not rest there, however,
for feelings of uncertainty about his action crept into his
heart.

Wanting to know whether what he did was right, and if

---

[1] *Al-Bukhari* 5663 and *Muslim* 1798.

wrong, whether he could make amends, Usâmah 🔹 gave an account of what had happened to the Messenger of Allâh 🔹.

«أَقَالَ: لَا إِلَهَ إِلَّا اللهُ وَقَتَلْتَهُ؟»

"Did you kill him even though he said, 'None has the right to be worshipped but Allâh'?" asked the Prophet 🔹.

"O Messenger of Allâh," said Usâmah, "he only said it because he feared my weapon (i.e., he only said to in order to safe his life)."

«أَفَلَا شَقَقْتَ عَنْ قَلْبِهِ حَتَّى تَعْلَمَ أَقَالَهَا أَمْ لَا؟»

"Should you not have split his heart in order to know whether he said it (from his heart) or not (i.e., since you cannot do that, you should have based your judgment on what his tongue had pronounced)?"[1]

The Prophet 🔹 invoked Allâh 🔹 to forgive Usâmah 🔹; also, he 🔹 ordered Usâmah 🔹 to free a slave (as a form of atonement); he did not, however, punish Usâmah 🔹 or ask him to pay blood money.

Usâmah bin Zaid's Counsel And Steadfast Faith

As the Muslims were returning from one of their military expeditions, 'Aishah 🔹 got left behind. The Muslim army had stopped for a short while on its way back to Al-Madinah. 'Aishah 🔹 left the camp in order to take care of some personal business. Upon returning, she realized that she had lost her bracelet. She wandered off in search of it, and by the time she returned, the Muslims had already

---

[1] *Al-Bukhari* 4269 and *Muslim* 96.

resumed their homeward-bound journey; everyone had simply assumed that 'Aishah ﵁ was among them. All alone now, she faced a very difficult predicament, but she was soon saved by one of the Muslims. That Muslim's job was to stay somewhat in the rear of the Muslim army in order to pick up any object that any soldier might inadvertently drop. He came across 'Aishah ﵁, dismounted from his riding animal, quietly moved to hold the animal by its rein, turned his face away while 'Aishah ﵁ mounted the animal, and then steered the animal, with 'Aishah ﵁ riding on it, towards Al-Madinah.

When they returned the next morning, one of the first people to see them was 'Abdullâh bin Ubai bin Salûl, the chief hypocrite of Al-Madinah. He immediately leveled an utterly false and vile accusation against them, saying, "They were together during the night. She was not saved from him, and he was not saved from her." Ibn Ubai's accusation quickly gained currency among Madinah's hypocrites. What is sad, however, is that even some sincere Muslims placed credence in Ibn Ubai's accusations.

For his part, the Prophet ﷺ was overcome by a great deal of sadness. 'Aishah ﵁ insisted that she was innocent, but she had no tangible proof that would help to exonerate her in the eyes of others. It was a most difficult time for everyone involved, including Abu Bakr ﵁, 'Aishah's father. The Prophet ﷺ spoke of this matter with two of his closest Companions ﵁, Companions ﵁ who were well-acquainted with the personal and family life of the Prophet ﷺ, namely, 'Ali bin Abi Tâlib ﵁ and Usâmah bin Zaid ﵁.

Usâmah ﵁ listened attentively as the Prophet ﷺ confided in him, telling him of the pain he ﷺ felt and of the accusations that people were leveling against the Mother of the

Believers, 'Aishah 🌸. When the Prophet ﷺ was finished explaining the situation as it stood, Usâmah 🌸 said, "O Messenger of Allâh, as for your family (wives), I know only good things about them. As for what the people say, it is a lie and completely false."

Throughout the entire ordeal, Usâmah 🌸 – as well as other Companions 🌸 – believed with certainty that 'Aishah 🌸 was pure, righteous, and chaste, and that she was completely innocent. And of course, he 🌸 was right. The ordeal finally came to an end when Allâh 🌸 revealed Verses of the Qur'ân that established 'Aishah's innocence.

A Dutiful Son

The value of a date-palm tree during the caliphate of 'Uthmân 🌸 increased to 1000 dirhams, a large amount at the time. Usâmah bin Zaid 🌸 betook himself to one of his date-palm trees and removed from it its syrup, which is a soft, white substance that is found at the highest point of the date-palm tree. When one removes that substance, one effectively destroys the value of the tree he takes it from.

Usâmah 🌸 then took the substance to his mother. When others learned of what Usâmah 🌸 had done, they were shocked and could not understand why he would purposefully ruin the value of an expensive tree. "What made you do this? You know that your tree was worth 1000 dirhams."

"My mother asked me for it (the syrup)," explained Usâmah 🌸. "And whenever she asks me for something that I am able to give, I always give it to her."

The Day of the Makkah Conquest

When the Prophet ﷺ rode into Makkah during the Makkah Conquest, he rode on his riding camel, Al-Qaswâ'; and seated behind him on Al-Qaswâ' was Usâmah bin Zaid ﷺ. It was a Friday morning, and the Messenger of Allâh ﷺ was wearing a black turban, its two ends hanging between his shoulders. He ﷺ was not attired in the non-stitched garment that a pilgrim wears. He ﷺ placed his head on his mount, showing humbleness to Allâh ﷻ, and then said, "O Allâh, indeed the (true, eternal, and good) life is the life of the Hereafter."[1]

Usâmah ﷺ related that, upon entering the Ka'bah, the Prophet ﷺ saw pictures. Usâmah ﷺ then repeatedly brought him water, which the Prophet ﷺ used to erase the pictures, all the while saying, "May Allâh fight those people who draw that which they do not create."

In Regard to Allâh's Set Limits, No Intercession is Accepted

During the Prophet's lifetime, a woman named Fâtimah bint Abul-Asad ﷺ was caught stealing. Sufficient proof was presented to establish her guilt, and so it was obvious that the Islamic ruling for stealing should be applied to her. However, there was one problem: Fâtimah bint Abul-Asad ﷺ was from the Banu Makhzûm tribe, one of the most honorable of tribes in Arabia. The leaders of Banu Makhzûm approached the Prophet ﷺ and offered to pay ransom money in order to save Fâtimah bint Abul-Asad from having her hand cut off.

---

[1] *Ahmad* 5/209, *An-Nasai'* 2909 and *Ibn Khuzaimah* 3005.

"Cut off her hand," was the simple reply of the Prophet ﷺ.
"We will ransom her [safety] for 500 dinars," they said.

«اقْطَعُوا يَدَهَا»

"Cut off her hand,"[1] said the Prophet ﷺ.

The leaders of Banu Makhzûm were deeply upset by the situation. They searched out for someone who could intercede to the Prophet ﷺ on their behalf. Someone suggested Usâmah bin Zaid 🌸, for if anyone had the courage to intercede in the said matter, it was Usâmah bin Zaid 🌸. After all, both Usâmah and his father 🌸 were close to and loved by the Prophet ﷺ.[2] And so they presented their case to Usâmah 🌸 and asked him to intercede on their behalf.

When the Prophet ﷺ saw Usâmah bin Zaid 🌸 approach, he ﷺ said:

«لَا تُكَلِّمُنِي يَا أُسَامَةُ، فَإِنَّ الْحُدُودَ إِذَا انْتَهَتْ إِلَيَّ فَلَيْسَ لَهَا مَتْرَكٌ، وَلَوْ كَانَتْ بِنْتُ مُحَمَّدٍ فَاطِمَةُ لَقَطَعْتُهَا . يَا أُسَامَةُ أَتُكَلِّمُنِي فِي حَدٍّ مِنْ حُدُودِ اللهِ تَعَالَى؟»

"Do not speak to me (regarding this matter), O Usâmah. Once a matter regarding Allâh's set limits (punishment for a crime) reaches me, no one can stop it from being executed.[3] *Had it been Fâtimah, the daughter of Muhammad (who was caught stealing), I would have cut her (hand) off. O Usâmah, do not speak to me (i.e., do not intercede to me) about a limit from the limits of Allâh*

---

[1] *Ahmad* 2/177, 178 and *Majma'* 6/276.
[2] *Al-Bukhari* 3475.
[3] *Al-Isabah* 8/270.

Ta'ala (the Exalted).''[1]

No sooner did Usâmah ﷺ see a change in the color of the Prophet's face than he felt regret for having come in the first place with the intention of trying to intercede.[2] "Ask (Allâh) to forgive me, O Messenger of Allâh," he ﷺ said.

Meanwhile, the people of Banu Makhzûm were nervously waiting for Usâmah ﷺ to come out, and when he did, they hurried to him and asked, "Did he accept your intercession."

"May Allâh have mercy on you," Usâmah ﷺ said. "The Messenger of Allâh ﷺ has just taught me a profound lesson."

The Messenger of Allâh ﷺ then stood up to deliver a sermon. First praising Allâh ﷻ, he ﷺ went on to say:

«أَمَّا بَعْدُ، فَإِنَّمَا أَهْلَكَ النَّاسَ قَبْلَكُمْ: أَنَّهُمْ كَانُوا إِذَا سَرَقَ فِيهِمُ الشَّرِيفُ تَرَكُوهُ، وَإِذَا سَرَقَ فِيهِمُ الضَّعِيفُ أَقَامُوا عَلَيْهِ الْحَدَّ، وَالَّذِي نَفْسُ مُحَمَّدٍ بِيَدِهِ! لَوْ أَنَّ فَاطِمَةَ بِنْتَ مُحَمَّدٍ سَرَقَتْ لَقَطَعْتُ يَدَهَا»

"As for what follows: The only cause that led to the destruction of the people who came before you is that, if a noble (person) among them stole, they would leave him; and if a weak person among them stole, they would execute upon him the legislated punishment. By the One Who has the soul of Muhammad in His Hand, were Fâtimah bint Muhammad to steal, I would cut off her

---

[1] *Al-Bukhari* 4304.

[2] *Al-Bukhari* 4304.

hand.''[1]

He ﷺ then gave Bilal bin Rabâh 🙵 the order to cut off Fâtimah bint Al-Aswad's hand.

Fâtimah bint Al-Aswad 🙵 later said, "O Messenger of Allâh, is there still an opportunity for me to repent?"

"Today, in relation to your sinning, you are just as you were on the day that your mother gave you birth (i.e., because of her repentance, as well as her punishment, her past sins were erased)." Then Allâh ﷻ revealed the Verse:

$$﴿فَمَن تَابَ مِنۢ بَعۡدِ ظُلۡمِهِۦ وَأَصۡلَحَ فَإِنَّ ٱللَّهَ يَتُوبُ عَلَيۡهِۚ إِنَّ ٱللَّهَ غَفُورٞ رَّحِيمٌ ٣٩﴾$$

"But whosoever repents after his crime and does righteous good deeds (by obeying Allâh), then verily, Allâh will pardon him (accept his repentance). Verily, Allâh is Oft-Forgiving, Most Merciful."[2]

Referring to Fâtimah bint Al-Aswad 🙵, the Messenger of Allâh ﷺ said:

«لِتَتُبْ هَذِهِ الْمَرْأَةُ إِلَى اللهِ وَرَسُولِهِ وَتَرُدَّ مَا تَأْخُذُ عَلَى الْقَوْمِ»

"Let this woman [return] to Allâh and His Messenger, and let her return what she took (stole) from the people."[3]

It was her right hand that Bilal 🙵 had cut off.

The Mother of the Believers, 'Aishah 🙵, said, "She performed a good repentance (i.e., she repented sincerely

---

[1] Al-Bukhari 4304.
[2] Qur'ân 5: 39.
[3] Reported by An-Nasai in Al-Kubrah 7376.

and mended her ways).'' Fâtimah bint Al-Aswad's punishment and all similar punishments in the Shari'ah are a form of purification for the sinner. Fâtimah ﴾ resumed her role in society; she married, frequently visited 'Aishah ﴿, and went with her problems to the Messenger of Allâh ﷺ.

Do You Enjoin People to do Good...

Allâh ﷻ said:

﴿أَتَأْمُرُونَ ٱلنَّاسَ بِٱلْبِرِّ وَتَنسَوْنَ أَنفُسَكُمْ وَأَنتُمْ تَتْلُونَ ٱلْكِتَٰبَ أَفَلَا تَعْقِلُونَ ٤٤﴾

"Enjoin you Al-Birr (piety and righteousness and each and every act of obedience to Allâh) on the people and you forget (to practise it) yourselves, while you recite the Scripture [the Taurat (Torah)]! Have you then no sense?''[1]

Usâmah bin Zaid ﴾ reported that, when this Verse was revealed, the Messenger of Allâh ﷺ said:

«يُؤْتَى بِالرَّجُلِ يَوْمَ الْقِيَامَةِ فَيُلْقَى فِي النَّارِ فَتَنْدَلِقُ – تَخْرُجُ بِسُرْعَةٍ – أَقْتَابُ – أَمْعَاءٌ جَمْعٌ وَمُفْرَدُهَا قَتَبٌ – بَطْنِهِ فَيَدُورُ بِهَا كَمَا يَدُورُ الْحِمَارُ بِالرَّحَى فَيَجْتَمِعُ إِلَيْهِ أَهْلُ النَّارِ فَيَقُولُونَ: يَا فُلَانُ، مَالَكَ؟ أَلَمْ تَكُنْ تَأْمُرُ بِالْمَعْرُوفِ وَتَنْهَى عَنِ الْمُنْكَرِ؟ فَيَقُولُ: بَلَى قَدْ كُنْتُ آمُرُ بِالْمَعْرُوفِ وَلَا آتِيهِ وَأَنْهَى عَنِ الْمُنْكَرِ وَآتِيهِ»

"A man will be brought on the Day of Resurrection and

---

[1] Qur'ân 2: 44.

will then be thrown into the Hellfire. His intestines will come out and fall down, and he will go around them just as a donkey goes around its grindstone (i.e., the post to which it is tied). The people of the Hellfire will gather around him and say, 'O so and so, didn't you used to enjoin good and forbid (others) from (doing) evil?' He will say, 'Yes, I used to enjoin good but not do it myself, and I used to forbid (others) from (doing) evil but I would do it myself.'"[1]

When the Messenger of Allâh ﷺ would go on a journey, he ﷺ would have one poor person remain in the company of two rich people, so that he could serve them; this way, the poor person could find a way of earning his upkeep. On one particular journey, the Prophet ﷺ united Salmân Al-Fârisi ☙ with two men in the manner just described.

When Salmân ☙ entered into the service of the two men, they said to him, "Go and ask the Prophet ﷺ to give us food and *Idâm* (*Idâm* refers to any food that is eaten with bread)." Salmân ☙ went to the Messenger of Allâh ﷺ, who said, "Go to Usâmah bin Zaid and say, 'If you have extra food...' and then ask him to give it (that leftover food) to you." Usâmah ☙ was the Prophet's treasurer.

"I don't have anything with me," is what Usâmah ☙ said when Salmân ☙ asked him if he had any extra food, and so Salmân ☙ returned to the two men and informed them about what had happened.

"Indeed, he did have (food) with him, but he was being miserly," said the two men. Salmân ☙ tried to procure food for the two men from other Companions ☙ of the Prophet

---

[1] *Al-Bukhari* 3267 and *Muslim* 2989.

ﷺ, but he couldn't find anything with them. Upon learning of how Salmân ؓ couldn't find any food, the two men said to one another, "Were we to send Salmân to a generous well (one that is filled with water), its water would sink down."

The two men then went to Usâmah ؓ to check whether he had any food, but they were met and stopped on the way by the Prophet ﷺ, who said:

«مَالِي أَرَى خُضْرَةَ اللَّحْمِ فِي أَفْوَاهِكُمَا؟»

"Why is it that I see the greenness of meat in your mouths?"

"O Prophet of Allâh," they said, "we have not eaten any meat today, nor anything else."

"To the contrary, you were busy eating the meat of Salmân and Usâmah (i.e., they were backbiting them)," said the Prophet ﷺ. This Verse was then revealed:

﴿يَٰٓأَيُّهَا ٱلَّذِينَ ءَامَنُواْ ٱجۡتَنِبُواْ كَثِيرٗا مِّنَ ٱلظَّنِّ إِنَّ بَعۡضَ ٱلظَّنِّ إِثۡمٞ وَلَا تَجَسَّسُواْ وَلَا يَغۡتَب بَّعۡضُكُم بَعۡضًا أَيُحِبُّ أَحَدُكُمۡ أَن يَأۡكُلَ لَحۡمَ أَخِيهِ مَيۡتٗا فَكَرِهۡتُمُوهُ﴾

"O you who believe! Avoid much suspicions, indeed some suspicions are sins. And spy not, neither backbite one another. Would one of you like to eat the flesh of his dead brother? You would hate it (so hate backbiting)."[1]

His Ranking Among the Muslims

Just before he died, the Messenger of Allâh ﷺ prepared an army that was to be headed by Usâmah bin Zaid ؓ. The

---

[1] Qur'ân 49: 12.

army was to march towards a place called Ubna, which was in Sham, the place wherein Usâmah's father, Zaid ﷺ, was martyred. Around the time that the army was preparing to leave, the Prophet's health took a turn for the worse: he developed a fever and a headache. On the following morning, the Prophet ﷺ handed the banner (that is given to the leader of the army) to Usâmah ﷺ and instructed him to fight in the name of Allâh ﷻ and in the way of Allâh ﷻ.

Many people from the *Muhâjirûn* and the *Ansâr* were taken aback by the Prophet's decision to appoint Usâmah ﷺ as leader of such an important military expedition. It was certainly a surprise to most, for Usâmah bin Zaid ﷺ was only 18 or 19 years old at the time. Some people verbally expressed their misgivings, "This young boy is being appointed over the *Muhâjirûn* ... and the *Ansâr*?"

News of what they said reached the Prophet ﷺ, and he ﷺ became very angry. Although he ﷺ was sick, he went out to address the Muslims. With a kind of bandage tied around his head, the Prophet ﷺ ascended the pulpit, praised Allâh ﷻ, and then said:

«أَمَّا بَعْدُ: أَيُّهَا النَّاسُ، فَمَا مَقَالَةٌ بَلَغَتْنِي عَنْ بَعْضِكُمْ فِي تَأْمِيرِي أُسَامَةَ، وَلَئِنْ طَعَنْتُمْ فِي تَأْمِيرِي أُسَامَةَ لَقَدْ طَعَنْتُمْ فِي إِمَارَتِي أَبَاهُ مِنْ قَبْلِهِ، وَأَيْمُ اللهِ إِنْ كَانَ لَخَلِيقًا بِالْإِمَارَةِ، وَإِنَّ ابْنَهُ مِنْ بَعْدِهِ لَخَلِيقٌ بِالْإِمَارَةِ، وَإِنْ كَانَ لَمِنْ أَحَبِّ النَّاسِ إِلَيَّ، وَإِنَّهُمَا مِظَنَّةٌ لِكُلِّ خَيْرٍ، فَاسْتَوْصُوا بِهِ خَيْرًا فَإِنَّهُ مِنْ خِيَارِكُمْ»

"As for what follows: O people, what is this saying that has reached me from some of you concerning my appointment of Usâmah as leader (of the Muslim army)? If you have attacked my decision to appoint

Usâmah as leader (of the army), then you have also attacked my decision to appoint his father before him (to the same post). And by Allâh, he was indeed worthy of being leader. And by Allâh, his son after him is indeed worthy of being leader. And indeed, he is from the most beloved of people to me. Indeed, both of them are most likely candidates for all that is good. So treat him (Usâmah ﷺ) well, for he is indeed from the best among you.''[1]

The Prophet ﷺ then descended from the pulpit and returned to his house.

But before Usâmah's army could begin its march towards Ash-Sham, the Prophet ﷺ died, which left the first *Khalifah* of Islam, Abu Bakr ﷺ, with a very important decision to make. After the Prophet ﷺ died, many of the neighboring Bedouin tribes apostatized. Add to that the problem of Musaylamah Al-Kadhdhâb and others who claimed to be prophets. A serious military conflict between the Muslims and the apostates was about to begin. With problems near the heart of the Muslim Nation, some Muslims suggested to Abu Bakr ﷺ that he did not send Usâmah's army to Ash-Sham, for the members of that army were needed for the new conflict that had suddenly arisen near home.

Abu Bakr ﷺ didn't see things that way; in fact, he became very angry at their suggestion and said, "By Allâh, for a bird to snatch me up is more beloved to me than for me to call back an army that the Messenger of Allâh ﷺ has sent." Having received his orders from the Khalifah ﷺ, Usâmah ﷺ led his army to Ash-Sham in what ended up being a short expedition, for they

---

[1] *Al-Bukhari* 4469, *Muslim* 2426, *Ahmad* 2/89 and *Ibn Sa'd* 4/49.

returned just two months later to Al-Madinah.[1]

The Caliphate of 'Umar ﷺ

'Umar bin Al-Khattâb ﷺ would allot an endowment of 5000 dirhams to Usâmah bin Zaid ﷺ, and only 2000 dirhams to his own son, 'Abdullâh ﷺ. Slightly stung by this distribution, 'Abdullâh bin 'Umar ﷺ said, "I have been deemed superior to Usâmah and have participated in important battles from which he was absent."

"Usâmah was more beloved to the Messenger of Allâh ﷺ than you were," said 'Umar ﷺ to his son. "And his father (Zaid ﷺ) was more beloved to the Messenger of Allâh ﷺ than your father was." Such was the just nature of 'Umar bin Al-Khattâb ﷺ: he gave preference to the beloved one of the Messenger of Allâh ﷺ over his own beloved one – his son, 'Abdullâh ﷺ.[2]

He ﷺ did not Take Sides During the Days of *Fitnah* (Trials, Tribulations, Internal Strife among the Muslims)

When a misunderstanding led to a huge *Fitnah* (trials, tribulations, internal strife among the Muslims) between 'Ali bin Abu Tâlib ﷺ and Mu'âwiyah bin Abi Sufyâh ﷺ, Usâmah ﷺ took no part in the battles that divided the ranks of the Muslims and that pitted Muslim against Muslim. Yet, wanting to express his love for 'Ali ﷺ, Usâmah ﷺ wrote him the following message: "Indeed, if you were to find yourself in between the jaws of a lion, I would love to enter into its mouth with you (i.e., that is how much I would be willing to

---

[1] *Ibn Sa'd* 4/50, and *Ibn Asakir* 8/45.
[2] *Ibn Sa'd* 4/52 and *At-Tirmidhi* 3813.

sacrifice), but I do not see this present situation in that light."

Indeed, Allâh ﷻ does not Love the *Al-Fâhish* or the *Al-Mutafahhish*

One day, while Usâmah bin Zaid ؓ was praying near the door of the Prophet ﷺ, Marwân bin Al-Hakam passed by and spoke harsh and mean words to Usâmah ؓ, going as far as supplicating against him.

"You have hurt me," said Usâmah ؓ. "And you are a *Fâhish* and a *Mutafahhish*, and I indeed heard the Messenger of Allâh ﷺ say, "Indeed, Allâh ﷻ despises the *Fâhish* (*Fâhish* is a person who utters vile words, who points out his brother's faults when he meets him), the *Mutafâhish* (*Mutafahish* is a person who does the things that a *Fâhish* does, but in an affected and intentional manner)."[1]

A Narrator of *Hadith*

Abu Hurairah and Ibn 'Abbâs ؓ were among the Companions who narrated *Hadith* narrations from Usâmah bin Zaid ؓ. Many *Tâbi'ûn* also narrated from Usâmah ؓ; Abu 'Uthmân An-Nahdi and Abu Wâ'il are two examples.

His Death

After years of traveling and living in different places – such as Al-Mazzah near Damascus and then Wâdi Al-Qura – Usâmah bin Zaid ؓ settled in Al-Madinah. In the year 54 H, he ؓ died in Al-Jurf. May Allâh be pleased with him.

---

[1] *At-Tabarani* 1/166 and *Majama'* 8/64,45.

Sa‘d bin Mu‘âdh رضي الله عنه

Sa'd bin Mu'âdh ﷺ

His Lineage

He is Sa'd bin Mu'âdh bin An-No'mân bin Imrau'l-Qais bin Zaid bin 'Abdul-'Ashhal bin Jusham bin Al-Hârith bin Al-'Aus Al-Ansâri Al-Ashhali. His mother is Kabshah bint Râfi'.

His *Kunyah*

His *Kunyah* is Abu 'Amr.

His Islam

Like many of Al-Madinah's inhabitants, Sa'd bin Mu'âdh ﷺ embraced Islam at the hands of Mus'ab bin 'Umair ﷺ. Sa'd ﷺ then went with Usaid bin Hudair ﷺ, who had embraced Islam just before he did, to the members of the Banu 'Abdul-Ashhal clan. Sa'd ﷺ and Usaid ﷺ presented the teachings of Islam to them and recited to them Verses of the Qur'ân. After this meeting was concluded, they all went together to destroy the idols that they had worshipped for their entire lives.

Bonds of Brotherhood

Sa'd bin Mu'âdh's assigned brother from the *Muhâjirûn* was Abu 'Ubaidah bin Al-Jarrâh ﷺ.

The Day of Badr

The original plan of the Muslims was to intercept Abu Sufyân's trading caravan. But with the coming of Quraish's army for battle, a course of action had to be decided upon, and so the Prophet ﷺ said:

«أَشِيرُوا عَلَيَّ أَيُّهَا النَّاسُ»

"O people, give me your counsel."

At first, some members of the *Muhâjirûn* came forward and spoke well, but the Prophet ﷺ was waiting for someone from the *Ansâr* to say something. This is because the *Ansâr* pledged, in the second pledge of Al-'Aqabah, to defend the Prophet ﷺ just as they would defend themselves and their families. They did not explicitly say that they would go and do battle outside of Al-Madinah. Therefore, the Prophet ﷺ needed to know whether the *Ansâr* would be willing to go out and face Quraish's army; preferably, he ﷺ wanted one of the leaders of the *Ansâr* to speak.

One of the leaders of the *Ansâr* did come forward then, and he was Sa'd bin Mu'âdh ﷺ. The Prophet ﷺ had just repeated his request: "O people, give me your counsel." Sa'd ﷺ said, "O Messenger of Allâh... by Allâh, it seems like you want us (i.e., the *Ansâr*) (to answer you)."

"Yes," said the Messenger of Allâh ﷺ.

"O Messenger of Allâh," began Sa'd, "We indeed have faith in you and believe you, and we bear witness that what you came with is the truth. And for that, we have given you our covenant and pledge to listen to and obey (all of your commands). So go forth, O Messenger of Allâh, to wherever you want to go, for we are with you. For by the One Who has sent you with the truth, were you to take us to this sea and then rush into it (to cross it), we would rush into it after you – not a single one of us would remain behind. And we do not dislike for you to meet our enemy with us tomorrow. Indeed, we are patient and steadfast in war, and truthful when (the two armies) meet (for battle). Perhaps Allâh will show you from us that which will be the delight of your eye (i.e., that which will please you immensely). So go forth with us, upon the blessing of Allâh." The Messenger of Allâh's face then began to radiate with happiness and joy. He ⛤ said, "Proceed forward and rejoice, for indeed, Allâh ⛤ has promised me one of two groups (i.e., either the caravan of Abu Sufyân or victory over Quraish's army). By Allâh, it is as if I am looking at the place where they will be killed."

Sa'd bin Mu'âdh ⛤ later went to the Prophet ⛤ and said, "O Prophet of Allâh, should we not build a trellis that you can stay in (and that can serve as the headquarters of the army) ... Then when we meet the enemy, if Allâh ⛤ honors us, and we come out victorious over our enemy, then that will be what we truly love and want. But if it is the other outcome (i.e., defeat) ... you can return to those (Muslims) who are behind us (in Al-Madinah). O Prophet of Allâh, as for some of the people whom you left behind, we do not love you more than they do, nor are we more obedient to you than they are. They have both an intention and a desire to perform *Jihâd*. Had they known that you will do battle, they would not have stayed behind. The only reason they stayed behind is that they thought you were simply going to intercept the caravan (and then return). Through them, Allâh will protect you. They will be sincere to you, and they will fight alongside you..."[1]

The Messenger of Allâh ﷺ praised Sa'd ﷺ, supplicated for him, and said, "Or Allâh will decree what is better than that, O Sa'd." The Prophet ﷺ was certain that Allâh ﷻ was going to grant him victory, for Allâh ﷻ promised him [victory over] one of the two groups (the caravan or the army of the Quraish). Since Abu Sufyân was able to flee with his caravan, there remained only the Quraish, and the Prophet ﷺ said that it was as if he saw the place wherein they were going to be killed.

The Prophet ﷺ implemented Sa'd's idea; a trellis was soon built on the top of a hill that overlooked the battlefield. As for Sa'd ﷺ, he had the honor of carrying the banner for the Aus tribe.

When the battle was over and the prisoners had been rounded up, the Prophet ﷺ consulted his Companions ﷺ concerning what they should do with the prisoners. Sa'd bin Mu'âdh ﷺ, who felt angry for the 13 years that his brothers and sisters were persecuted in Makkah, said, "O Messenger of Allâh, kill them and do not take the ransom (money that will ensure their release)."

The Day of Uhud

It is important to mention here that, when many people began to flee from the battlefield on the Day of Uhud, Sa'd bin Mu'âdh ﷺ was one of the few who remained firm alongside the Messenger of Allâh ﷺ.

---

[1] Ibn Is-haq in *Sirah* 2/620. See *Faqh As-Sirah* by Albani 226.

The Day of Al-Khandaq

It is related that, during the Battle of Al-Khandaq, 'Aishah ﷺ was with *Umm* (the Mother of) Sa'd bin Mu'âdh ﷺ in the castle of Banu Al-Hârithah. Of course the women had to be kept at a safe distance from the front lines. While they were inside, Sa'd ﷺ passed by; 'Aishah ﷺ said to Umm Sa'd ﷺ, "O mother of Sa'd, I wish that the armor of Sa'd would cover him more completely." 'Aishah ﷺ had reason to fear, for shortly thereafter Sa'd ﷺ was struck by an arrow where he was not protected by armor. The man who fired the arrow was Ibn (son of) Al-'Ariqah. As he released the arrow from his bow, he said, "Take this, and I am Ibn Al-'Ariqah." Here, the man was saying that he was the son of a woman named 'Ariqah. *'Ariqah* comes from the word *'Araq*, which means sweat; she was given that name because her sweat exuded a sweet fragrance. Quite fittingly, then, the Messenger of Allâh ﷺ called back to him, "May Allâh make your face sweat in the Hellfire!" Though he was injured, Sa'd ﷺ was still in high spirits, which we can clearly see from what he said after he was wounded: "O Allâh, if You will make the war against the Quraish continue for some more time, then make me stay (alive) for it. For indeed, there are no people that I would love to fight more than the people that inflicted harm upon Your Messenger ﷺ, expelled him (from his homeland), and disbelieved in him."[1]

---

[1] *Ahmad* 6/141, 142 and *Al-Bukhari* 4122.

A Meeting To Consult With Sa'd bin Mu'âdh and Sa'd bin 'Ubâdah ﷺ

During the same battle, which was more a drawn out besiegement than an actual battle, the Muslims were going through difficult times for the very fact that the siege was lasting so long. On the other side of the trenches, a huge army was waiting for the Muslims to give in. The army consisted of the Quraish and many other tribes, which is why they were called the confederates.

One of the enemy tribes was the Ghatafân tribe, which was headed by 'Uyainah bin Hisn Al-Fazâri and Al-Hârith bin 'Auf Al-Murri. The Prophet ﷺ invited them to negotiate terms; one solution, which pleased 'Uyainah and Al-Hârith, was that in return for the Ghatafân tribe leaving without fighting, the Muslims would thereafter give them one-third of Al-Madinah's crops. But the Prophet ﷺ did not want to finalize this agreement without first consulting with his Companions ﷺ, and so he called the two main leaders of the *Ansâr*: Sa'd bin Mu'âdh ﷺ, leader of the Aus tribe, and Sa'd bin 'Ubâdah ﷺ, leader of the Khazraj tribe. After the Prophet ﷺ consulted them, S'ad bin Mu'âdh ﷺ gave the following reply: "O Messenger of Allâh, when we and these people (the Ghatafân tribe) associated partners with Allâh in worship, when we worshipped idols, when we neither worshipped Allâh nor knew Him, they (the Ghatafân) had no ambition to eat even a single one of our fruits, unless they received it in the capacity of guests or buyers. So now that Allâh has honored us with Islam, guided us to it, and honored us with you, will we simply give them our wealth? By Allâh, we have no need of this (of such an agreement). By Allâh, we will give them nothing save the sword, until Allâh judges between us and them."

Then, raising his voice so that 'Uyainah bin Hisn and Al-Hârith bin 'Auf could clearly hear what he was saying, the Messenger of Allâh ﷺ said:

«اِرْجِعَا بَيْنَنَا وَبَيْنَكُمُ السَّيْفُ»

"Return, for between us and you is the sword."[1]

The siege continued and Sa'd 🙏 needed to be nursed back to health, for the arrow had done its damage. The Messenger of Allâh ﷺ ordered for Sa'd bin Mu'âdh 🙏 to be treated in the tent of Rafidah Al-Asdiyyah, which wasn't far from where the Prophet ﷺ was, so that he could visit him frequently.

Another problem then arose for the Muslims. Not only were the confederate armies threatening them from the north, the Banu Quraizah tribe now threatened them from the south. When the Prophet ﷺ first arrived in Al-Madinah, he signed a peace pact with the Banu Quraizah tribe; one of the terms of the pact was that, if the Muslims were to come under attack by an outside force, Banu Quraizah would defend them, and vice versa. But during the Battle of Khandaq, the Jews of Banu Quraizah blatantly violated the terms of the pact, treacherously agreeing with the confederate armies to side with them. They were taking their chances by betraying the Muslims, but they were confident that they would win out in the end; after all, the Quraish had come with 12,000 fighters and were sure to win. When Sa'd bin Mu'âdh 🙏 learned of their treachery, he 🙏 said, "O Allâh, do not make me die until I see that which pleases me regarding Banu Quraizah (i.e., that they get what they deserve)."[2]

---

[1] Abdur-Razzaq in *Al-Musannaf* 9737 and Ibn Hisham in *As-Sirah* 3/234.
[2] *Ahmad* 6/141, *Ibn Sa'd* 3/322, 324 and see *As-Siyar* 1/282.

Sa'd's Supplication Answered, and a Ruling that is Confirmed from above the Seven Heavens

Allâh ﷻ answered Sa'd's supplication: The confederates were forced to flee after Allâh ﷻ sent a very violent wind that wreaked havoc on their camp. Their lamps became extinguished, their pots flipped over, and their tents were uprooted. They all fled, leaving Banu Quraizah behind them. The confederate armies might have taken risks, but the real gamblers in this story were the people of Banu Quraizah; they felt that the odds were stacked so heavily against the Muslims that there would be no harm in betraying them. The enemies of Allâh plan, but Allâh ﷻ is the best of planners.

The leaders of Banu Quraizah were not naïve; they knew that what they had done was unforgivable. Instead of helping the Muslims in their hour of need, which was they had agreed to do in a signed pact, they betrayed the Muslims and tried to help bring about their destruction. And so the people of Banu Quraizah closed all of their windows, doors, and gates, and shut themselves up inside of their castles.

When the Muslims besieged them, the only option they had was to surrender. Since a judgment had to be made regarding their case, the Prophet ﷺ asked them to choose any of his Companions ﷺ to issue a judgment in the matter. They chose Sa'd bin Mu'âdh ﷺ.

"Issue a ruling regarding their case, O Sa'd," said the Prophet ﷺ.

"I rule," began Sa'd ﷺ, "that their men be killed, their wealth be taken as booty, their children and women be taken as captives, and their homes be given to the *Muhâjirûn* and not to (anyone from) the *Ansâr*."

"You have issued judgment upon them with the same judgment that Allâh issued from above the seven heavens." And that is how the above-mentioned supplication of Sa'd ﷺ was answered.

The Death of Sa'd bin Mu'âdh ﷺ

Sa'd bin Mu'âdh ﷺ was 37 years old when he died. Upon his death, Sa'd's mother, Kabshah bint Râfi' ﷺ, stood up, cried, and recited a verse of poetry, in which she expressed her grief.

The Prophet ﷺ said:

«لَا تَزِيدِي عَلَى هَذَا، كَانَ وَاللهِ! – مَا عَلِمْتُ – حَازِمًا وَفِي أَمْرِ اللهِ قَوِيًّا»

"Do not do more than that, for by Allâh, he was, as you know, resolute and strong regarding Allâh's Command (decree, order)."[1]

According to the end of this *Mursal* narration, he ﷺ then said:

«كُلُّ نَائِحَةٍ كَاذِبَةٍ إِلَّا أُمَّ سَعْدٍ»

"Every Nâihah (a woman who weeps loudly when someone dies and expresses her grief in a plaintive and complaining manner) is a liar except for the mother of Sa'd."[2]

When the Prophet ﷺ saw tears practically drowning

---

[1] *At-Tabarani* 5327 and *Al-Majma'* 6/139.
[2] *Ibn Sa'd* 3/326, 328. See *Al-Matalib Al-Aliyah* 843.

Kabshah's face, he ﷺ said:

«أَلَا يَرْقَأُ دَمْعُكَ وَيَذْهَبُ حُزْنُكِ؟ فَإِنَّ ابْنَكِ أَوَّلُ مَنْ ضَحِكَ اللهُ لَهُ
وَاهْتَزَّ لَهُ الْعَرْشُ»

"Will not your tears dry up and your grief go away? For indeed, your son was the first person for whom Allâh laughed. Also, the Throne shook for him (as is mentioned in another Hadith)."[1]

When the bier of Sa'd bin Mu'âdh's body was lifted, the hypocrites said, "Indeed, how very light his corpse is!" They said this with bitter hatred in their hearts, hatred that resulted from Sa'd's judgment regarding the Banu Quraizah tribe. In response to their derision, the Prophet ﷺ later explained why his corpse was so light to carry:

«إِنَّ الْمَلَائِكَةَ كَانَتْ تَحْمِلُهُ»

"Indeed, it was the angels who were carrying him."[2]

---

[1] At-Tabarani in *Al-Kabir* 5344, *AL-Majma'* 9/309 Al-Hakim in *Mustadrak* 3/306, *Ibn Sa'd* 3/332 and see *Al-Bukhari* 3803, *Muslim* 2467.

[2] *At-Tirmidhi* 3849, *Al-Hakim* 3/207 and *At-Tabarani* 5345.

Naufal bin Mu'âwiyah ﷺ

Naufal bin Mu'âwiyah ﷺ

His Lineage

He is Naufal bin Mu'âwiyah bin 'Amr Ad-Dili; however, some say that his lineage can be traced back as follows: Naufal bin Mu'âwiyah bin 'Amr Ad-Dili. The disagreement is limited to the name of his grandfather, so he is, according to both views, from the descendents of Ad-Dil, who was from the Kinânah tribe. Ad-Dil was the son of Bakr, who was the son of 'Abd-Manât, who in turn was the son of Kinânah.

His Islam

When the confederate armies returned from their abortive attempt to destroy the Muslims in Al-Madinah, there was one subject on the lips of everyone: the violent wind and the cold night that forced the confederate armies to return home and abandon the siege that had lasted for about a month. The violent winds caused their tents to be uprooted, their lamps to extinguish, and their pots to turn over on the ground. What made them feel so bitter was that they had come ever so close to destroying the Prophet ﷺ and his Companions ﷺ. Just before the night of the violent wind, the Banu Quraizah tribe broke their pact with the Muslims, which almost all but guaranteed the victory of the confederate armies. Imagine, then, the bitter disappointment they felt when their plans became thwarted. The timing of it all could not have been coincidental, which is why some people began to say, "He (the Prophet ﷺ) is a man who is protected (by Allâh ﷻ)."

Nauful bin Mu'âwiyah heard someone say this, and he began to contemplate the events that had taken place. How, he thought, could an army of 12,000 fail to defeat an army of 3 000? Why did the violent wind come just when victory was in their grasp, just after Banu Quraizah, through treacherous means, practically ensured their victory? Nauful bin Mu'âwiyah soon found himself climbing his mount with the intention of heading towards Al-Madinah. After he arrived there, and after the Prophet ﷺ recited for him the Qur'ân and explained to him the teachings of Islam, Nauful ؓ forthwith found that his tongue was uttering the Testimony of Truth (I bear witness that none has the right to be worshipped but Allâh and that Muhammad is the Messenger of Allâh).

The Makkah Conquest

When the Quraish blatantly violated the Treaty of Al-Hudaybiyyah, they, or at least the wiser ones among them, realized that they had made a serious mistake. Abu Sufyân immediately set out for Al-Madinah to try and bring calm to a situation that was getting tenser by the moment, but he returned to Makkah without having achieved his aim. Although they realized that they had made a serious blunder, the Quraish did not expect the Muslims to come and attack them in Makkah. This was well, for the Prophet ﷺ did not want them to know that the Muslims were coming to conquer Makkah. After taking all possible precautions to keep the expedition a secret, the Prophet ﷺ said:

$$«اللَّهُمَّ خُذْ عَلَى أَسْمَاعِهِمْ وَأَبْصَارِهِمْ فَلَا يَرَوْنَا إِلَّا بَغْتَةً وَلَا يَسْمَعُونَ بِنَا إِلَّا فَجْأَةً»$$

"O Allâh, block their hearing and sight (i.e., keep our plans hidden from the Quraish), so that they do not see us until we come upon them by surprise, and so that they do not hear us except by surprise (upon a sudden, when the army is about to enter Makkah)."[1]

Naufal bin Mu'âwiyah ☜ narrated that, when the Messenger of Allâh ﷺ was entering Makkah, Abu Bakr ☜ rode beside him, speaking to him and reciting "The Victory Chapter" of the Qur'ân:

$$﴿إِنَّا فَتَحْنَا لَكَ فَتْحًا مُبِينًا ۝﴾$$

"Verily, We have given you (O Muhammad ﷺ) a manifest victory."[2]

When the Prophet ﷺ reached the Ka'bah, he ﷺ made seven circuits around it while seated on his mount.

Once the Muslims entered Makkah, one of the first and most important tasks was to destroy the idols that were inside or near the Ka'bah. It was not a small task, for there were a total of 360 idols, one for each Arab sub-tribe; what made matters even more difficult was that the foot of each idol was tied down with lead. The Prophet ﷺ came prepared

---

[1] Al-Bayhaqi in *Ad-Dla'il* 4/9-12, *Al-Majma'* 6/164 and *Ibn Is-haq* 4/39, 40.
[2] *Qur'ân* 48: 1.

with a huge rod. One by one, he smashed the idols, all the
while saying:

﴿وَقُلْ جَآءَ ٱلْحَقُّ وَزَهَقَ ٱلْبَٰطِلُ إِنَّ ٱلْبَٰطِلَ كَانَ زَهُوقًا ۝﴾

*"The Truth has come and Bâtil (falsehood, i.e., Satan or
polytheism, etc.) has vanished. Surely! Bâtil is ever bound
to vanish."*[1]

The Freed Ones

After giving a short speech that shed light on the rulings for
certain legislations, the Prophet ﷺ said:

«يَا مَعْشَرَ قُرَيْشٍ، إِنَّ اللهَ قَدْ أَذْهَبَ عَنْكُمْ نَخْوَةَ الْجَاهِلِيَّةِ وَتَعَظُّمَهَا
بِالآبَاءِ، النَّاسُ مِنْ آدَمَ، وَآدَمُ مِنْ تُرَابٍ»

*"O people of Quraish, Allâh has indeed removed from you
the Nakhwah (things that are boasted over) of Jâhiliyyah
(Pre-Islamic days of ignorance) and the glorification that
is bestowed upon some by dint of their fathers (noble
lineages). People are from Adam, and Adam is from dirt."*

He ﷺ then recited this saying of Allâh ﷻ:

﴿يَٰٓأَيُّهَا ٱلنَّاسُ إِنَّا خَلَقْنَٰكُم مِّن ذَكَرٍ وَأُنثَىٰ وَجَعَلْنَٰكُمْ شُعُوبًا وَقَبَآئِلَ لِتَعَارَفُوٓاْ إِنَّ
أَكْرَمَكُمْ عِندَ ٱللَّهِ أَتْقَىٰكُمْ إِنَّ ٱللَّهَ عَلِيمٌ خَبِيرٌ ۝﴾

*"O mankind! We have created you from a male and a
female, and made you into nations and tribes, that you
may know one another. Verily, the most honourable of
you with Allâh is that (believer) who has At-Taqwa [i.e.,*

---

[1] *Qur'ân* 17: 81. Ibn Hisham in *As-Sirah* 4/59 and in *Muslim* as is it 1780,
same also in *Al-Bukhari* 4288.

one of the Muttaqûn (pious)]. Verily, Allâh is All-Knowing, All-Aware.''[1]

Addressing the Quraish, the Prophet ﷺ said:

«مَاذَا تَقُولُونَ وَمَاتَظُنُّونَ أَنِّي فَاعِلٌ فِيكُمْ؟»

"What do you say, and what do you think I will do with you?"

For thirteen years, the leaders of the Quraish ruthlessly persecuted the Muslims. Even when the Muslims left Makkah, the Quraish didn't leave them alone. They stole the wealth that the Muslims had left behind. And still they were not content and couldn't let matters rest; instead, they waged an all out war against the Muslims in Al-Madinah, trying their utmost to destroy them. Now that the Prophet ﷺ had the upper hand, and they were at his mercy, it was a most fitting question that the Prophet ﷺ asked, "What do you think I will do with you?" Despite all that they did, they knew that the Prophet ﷺ was merciful and forgiving, and so they said, "You will do good by us." One of them said, "We speak good things (about you) and we think good [things about you (i.e., that you will have mercy on us)]. You are a noble brother, the son of a noble brother, and you now have the upper hand (to do as you please with us)."

The Prophet of mercy ﷺ said, "I say what my brother Yousuf said:

﴿لَا تَثۡرِيبَ عَلَيۡكُمُ ٱلۡيَوۡمَۖ يَغۡفِرُ ٱللَّهُ لَكُمۡۖ وَهُوَ أَرۡحَمُ ٱلرَّٰحِمِينَ ٩٢﴾

"No reproach on you this day, may Allâh forgive you, and He is the Most Merciful of those who show mercy!"[2]

---

[1] Qur'ân 49: 13.
[2] Qur'ân 12: 92.

The Prophet ﷺ then said:

«اذْهَبُوا فَأَنْتُمُ الطُّلَقَاءُ»

"Go, for you are the freed ones."[1]

The Day of Hunain

The people of Hawâzin and Thaqif literally panicked when the Messenger of Allâh ﷺ and the Muslims conquered Makkah. They feared that the Muslim army was now going to march towards them, and so the two tribes united their forces and prepared to attack first. Whether it was arrogance or self-deception, or both, they began to say to one another, "By Allâh, Muhammad and his Companions have faced a people (an enemy) who do not know how to fight."

As soon as the Prophet ﷺ heard about their plans to attack, he too quickly assembled an army to go out and meet them. This army consisted of 2,000 men from the 'freed ones' mentioned above; therefore, these were new Muslims; and 10,000 Companions ﷺ who had set out with him from Al-Madinah.

The Muslims continued to march until they reached the Hunain valley. The Hawâzin and Thaqif tribes had arrived before the Muslims; in fact, they tried to hide themselves on both sides of the valley with the intention of ambushing the Muslims. Their plan was actually quite effective at first, for they attacked with a great deal of skill, and the Muslims were genuinely taken by surprise.

They first sprayed the Muslims with arrows, and then they

---

[1] *At-Tabari* 3/60,61, *Ibn Is-haq* 4/55, and see *Ahmad* 2/11 and *Al-Waqidi* 2/836.

raced down towards them with their swords. The Muslims began to scatter about in a confused manner, and the 'freed ones' of Makkah were the first to flee, with some of them saying to one another, "Forsake him, for this is his time (to face defeat)." The other Muslims began to follow them in a desperate attempt to escape, but the Prophet 🕮 maintained his position and began to call out:

«يَا أَنْصَارَ اللهِ وَأَنْصَارَ رَسُولِهِ، أَنَا عَبْدُاللهِ وَرَسُولُهُ، أَيْنَ أَيُّهَا النَّاسُ؟ هَلُمُّوا إِلَيَّ، أَنَا رَسُولُ اللهِ، أَنَا مُحَمَّدُ بْنُ عَبْدِاللهِ»

"O helpers of Allâh, O helpers of His Messenger. I am the slave of Allâh and His Messenger. Where are you going, O people! Come to me. I am the Messenger of Allâh. I am Muhammad bin (son of) 'Abdullâh."[1]

Naufal bin Mu'âwiyah 🕮 later recounted, "Al-'Abbâs bin 'Abdul-Muttalib 🕮 was holding onto the rein of the mule that belonged to the Messenger of Allâh 🕮. Al-'Abbâs 🕮 was a huge man with a roaring voice. When the Prophet 🕮 saw that the people did not look around (but instead continued to flee), he 🕮 said:

«يَاعَبَّاسُ، اصْرُخْ: يَا مَعْشَرَ الْأَنْصَارِ، يَا مَعْشَرَ أَصْحَابِ السَّمُرَةِ – شَجَرَةُ الطَّلْحِ وَهِيَ الشَّجَرَةُ الَّتِي كَانَتْ عِنْدَهَا بَيْعَةُ الرِّضْوَانِ يَوْمَ الْحُدَيْبِيَّةِ –»

"O 'Abbâs, scream out: O people of the Ansâr, O people of As-Samarah (i.e., the At-Talh Tree; it was under the At-Talh Tree that the Muslims made the Ar-Ridwân pledge on the Day of Al-Hudaibiyyah)."

Al-'Abbâs's voice reached the ears of the *Ansâr*, and this was

---

[1] *At-Tabari* 3/74 and see *Ahmad* 3/279 and *Al-Baihaqi* 5/129.

their reply: "We are coming to you in response to your call; here we are coming to you in response to your call."

The *Ansâr* gathered themselves around the Prophet ﷺ and fought alongside one another with such harmony and coordination that they were like the different body parts of a single fighter. It is not surprising that they were able to coordinate so well in an impromptu manner, for they had already fought many battles alongside one another. Now the battle had truly begun in earnest.

It was a tough battle, but in the end Allâh ﷺ forced defeat upon the polytheists, and the leaders of Hawâzin and Thaqif hurried back to Tâif and shut themselves up in one of their fortresses. But before doing so, they filled it with enough supplies to last them for an entire year. They took this precaution because they were confident that the Messenger of Allâh ﷺ was going to come after them, especially since it was they who were the first to show enmity.

And in fact, the Messenger of Allâh ﷺ did make the short trip from Hunain to Tâ'if, where he ﷺ and the Muslims besieged the enemy. Arrows were fired down upon them from on top of the fortress, and a number of Companions ﷺ were consequently wounded – such as 'Abdullâh bin Abu Bakr ﷺ, Sa'id bin Sa'id bin Al-'Aas ﷺ, and Thâbit bin Al-Ajda' Al-Ansâri ﷺ. The Muslims repeatedly tried and failed to break through the fortress, and so the Prophet ﷺ decided to make camp at some distance from the fortress, so as to remain outside of the shooting range of Thaqif and Hawâzin's archers.

On the fourth day of the siege, the Prophet ﷺ called out, "Any slave that comes down from the fortress and comes out to us, is a free man." 23 of Thaqif and Hawâzin's slaves made their way out of the fortress, thus gaining their freedom.

But the siege was no way near ending, and so 'Uyainah bin Hisn Al-Fazâri asked the Messenger of Allâh ﷺ permission to enter the fortress and to invite the people of Thaqif to Islam. Having obtained the Prophet's permission, 'Uyainah entered the fortress and said, "Remain firm in your fortress." He told them not to give up so easily.

When 'Uyainah returned to the Muslim camp, the Prophet ﷺ asked him, "O 'Uyainah, what did you say to them?"

"I told them to embrace Islam ... I warned them about the Hellfire and guided them to the way that leads to Paradise."

"You have lied," said the Prophet ﷺ. "All that you told them to do was to: remain firm in your fortress." 'Uyainah was dumbfounded; there were no Muslims in the fortress, so how could the Prophet ﷺ have found out about what he said? 'Uyainah ﷺ fell down to his knees and said regretfully, "You have spoken the truth, O Messenger of Allâh. I repent to Allâh for what I did, and I return to you (in obedience and asking for your pardon)."

The Counsel of Nauful bin Mu'âwiyah Ad-Dili ﷺ

As the Muslims saw from their first attempt, it was going to be very difficult to fight their way into the fortress. They could continue with their siege, but the besieged had enough supplies to last them for an entire year. So the Muslims could either try to get into the practically impenetrable fortress, wait outside for an entire year, or leave. When the Messenger of Allâh ﷺ consulted him in the matter, Nauful bin Mu'âwiyah ﷺ said, "O Messenger of Allâh, when a fox is in a hole, if you stand over it, you will get it. And if you leave it (where it is), it won't hurt you."

The Messenger of Allâh ﷺ then ordered 'Umar bin Al-Khattâb ﷺ to announce that they were leaving, but the people disliked the idea, saying, "How can we leave when we have not yet been granted victory?"

"Then go and fight," said the Messenger of Allâh ﷺ. They rushed towards the fortress, but no sooner did they come into the firing range of Thaqif's archers than they were bombarded by arrows that were falling like raindrops during heavy rainfall. Many of the Muslims were consequently injured.

When the Prophet ﷺ repeated his previous command, "Indeed, we are leaving, *In Shâ Allâh*," the Muslims submitted joyfully this time, and the Prophet ﷺ smiled when he ﷺ saw how quickly they changed their minds.[1]

With the Messenger of Allâh ﷺ

When the situation calmed down after the Makkah Conquest, Nauful bin Mu'âwiyah ﷺ returned with the Prophet ﷺ to Al-Madinah. In fact, he settled down there, having purchased a home in the district of the Banu Ad-Dil clan. Now that he embraced Islam, he wanted to stay as close as possible to the Prophet ﷺ, proving the old maxim that it is never too late to learn.[2] He ﷺ was sixty years old at the time, and he lived until the ripe age of 120 (100 according to some accounts). The year after he moved to Al-Madinah, 9 H, Nawful bin Mu'âwiyah ﷺ performed *Hajj* with Abu Bakr ﷺ.

Because Nauful ﷺ lived in Al-Madinah for about the last 2 years of the Prophet's life, he was able to witness many

---

[1] *Al-Bukhari* 4325 and *Muslim* 1778.
[2] *Tahdhibul-Kamal* 30/70.

sayings and deeds of the Prophet ﷺ. One day, while Naufal ﷺ was sitting down in the *Masjid* with some of the Prophet's Companions ﷺ, one of them mentioned that the people of Fâris had crowned Kisrah's daughter to be their ruler. The Messenger of Allâh ﷺ then said:

«لَنْ يُفْلِحَ قَوْمٌ وَلَّوْا أَمْرَهُمُ امْرَأَةً»

"No people prosper when they appoint a woman over their affairs (i.e., when they appoint a woman to be their leader)."[1]

On another occasion, the Prophet ﷺ said, "*Az-Zuhd* (seeking only those worldly possessions and pleasures that are basic necessities) in this world brings comfort and peace to the heart and body. Being desirous of it (i.e., desirous of superfluous worldly pleasures and possessions) brings fatigue to the heart and body."

A man once came to Al-Madinah and asked to be directed to the Messenger of Allâh ﷺ. 'Abdur-Rahmân bin Abu Bakr ﷺ pointed out the Prophet ﷺ, and the man then went to him and said, "O Messenger of Allâh, guide me to a deed that, if I do it, Allâh and the people will love me."

The Prophet ﷺ said:

«ازْهَدْ فِي الدُّنْيَا يُحِبَّكَ اللهُ، وَازْهَدْ فِيمَا أَيْدِي النَّاسِ يُحِبَّكَ النَّاسُ»

"Seek little (only what is necessary) from the world, and Allâh will love you. Seek little from what is in the hands of people, and the people will love you."[2]

On another occasion, Thaubân ﷺ asked, "O Prophet of

---

[1] *Al-Bukhari* 4425.
[2] *Ibn Majah* 4102, Al-Hakim in *Mustadrak* 4/313.

Allâh, what (amount) is deemed sufficient for me from this world?"

The Prophet ﷺ said:

«مَاسَدَّ جُوعَتَكَ، وَوَارَى عَوْرَتَكَ، وَإِنْ كَانَ لَكَ بَيْتٌ يُظِلُّكَ فَذَاكَ، وَإِنْ كَانَ لَكَ دَابَّةٌ فَبَخٍّ»

"(The amount that) removes your hunger and covers (in terms of clothes) your private parts. And if you have a house that provides you with shade, then that is fine. And if you have a riding animal, then that is excellent."[1]

That we should not run after worldly things does not mean that possessions are not important. To the contrary, it is of utmost importance for one to strive to earn lawful sustenance for himself and his family. A man once went to the Messenger of Allâh ﷺ and said, "O Messenger of Allâh, suppose that a man comes with the intention of (forcefully and wrongfully) taking my wealth?"

"Then do not give him your wealth," said the Prophet ﷺ.

"Suppose that he fights me," said the man.

"(Then) fight him," said the Prophet ﷺ.

"Suppose that he kills me."

"Then you are a martyr," said the Prophet ﷺ.

"Suppose that I end up killing him," said the man.

"(Then) he is in the Hellfire."[2]

It is related that the Prophet ﷺ said:

«تَعَوَّذُوا بِاللهِ مِنْ جُبِّ الْحُزْنِ»

---

[1] At-Tabarani in *Al-Awsat*. See *Al-Majma'* 10/254 and *Shu'bil- Iman* by Al-Baihaqi 9769-9872.

[2] *Muslim* 1401.

"Seek refuge with Allâh from Jubb Al-Huzn."

"And what is Jubb Al-Huzn?" asked 'Abdur-Rahmân bin Abu Bakr ﷺ and Abu Hurairah ﷺ.

"It is a valley in the Hellfire," said the Prophet ﷺ.

«وَادٍ فِي جَهَنَّمَ، تَتَعَوَّذُ مِنْهُ جَهَنَّمُ كُلَّ يَوْمٍ أَرْبَعَمِائَةِ مَرَّةٍ يَدْخُلُهُ الْقُرَّاءُ الْمُرَاءُونَ بِأَعْمَالِهِمْ، وَإِنَّ مِنْ أَبْغَضِ الْقُرَّاءِ إِلَى اللهِ الَّذِينَ يَزُورُونَ الْأُمَرَاءَ»

"The Hellfire itself seeks refuge from it (from that valley) 400 times a day. The Qurra' (reciters of the Qur'ân) who do their (good) deeds for show will enter it. And indeed, from the most despised of Qurra' to Allâh ﷺ are the ones that visit the leaders (i.e., those that go to leaders in order to curry favor with them)."[1]

It is also related that the Prophet ﷺ said:

«إِنَّ اللهَ تَعَالَى يَقُولُ: أَنَا خَيْرُ شَرِيكٍ، فَمَنْ أَشْرَكَ مَعِيَ شَيْئًا فَهُوَ لِشَرِيكِي، يَا أَيُّهَا النَّاسُ أَخْلِصُوا أَعْمَالَكُمْ لله، فَإِنَّ اللهَ لَا يَقْبَلُ مِنَ الْأَعْمَالِ إِلَّا مَا خَلَصَ لَهُ، وَلَا تَقُولُوا: هَذَا لله وَلِلرَّحِمِ، فَإِنَّهُ لِلرَّحِمِ وَلَيْسَ لله مِنْهُ شَيْءٌ»

"Indeed Allâh ﷺ says: "I am the best of partners: For whosoever associates a partner with Me in anything, then it (the act of worship in which Shirk is committed) is for My partner."' The Prophet ﷺ went on to say, "O people, make your deeds pure and sincere for Allâh; for indeed, Allâh accepts only those deeds that are performed purely

---

[1] *At-Tirmidhi* 2383, *Ibn Majah* 256 and Al-Baihaqi in *Ba'th wan-Nushûr* 481 and Al-Mundhiri graded it *Hasan* 5379.

*and sincerely for Him. And do not say, 'This is for Allâh
and for Ar-Rahim (ties of family relation), for (when you
say that) it is indeed for Ar-Rahim, and nothing from it is
for Allâh (i.e., by associating partners with Allâh in
worship, your deed is entirely for the partner you set up
alongside Allâh, even if you intended Allâh ﷻ partly
thereby)."*[1]

Once, when the Prophet ﷺ asked about Mu'âdh bin Jabal ﷺ,
someone answered, "He is gone to fulfill the need of so and
so."

The Prophet ﷺ said:

«إِنَّ للهِ عِبَادًا خَلَقَهُمْ لِحَوَائِجِ النَّاسِ، فَقَضَى حَوَائِجَ النَّاسِ عَلَى
أَيْدِيهِمْ، أُولَئِكَ آمِنُونَ مِنْ فَزَعِ يَوْمَ الْقِيَامَةِ»

*"Indeed, Allâh has slaves whom He created for the needs
of people (i.e., who help people when they are in need),
whereby He fulfills the needs of people at their hands.
Those (i.e., those who help others when they need help) are
safe from the terror of the Day of Resurrection."*[2]

In another narration, the Prophet ﷺ said:

«مَنْ أَعَانَ أَخَاهُ الْمَضْطَرَّ ثَبَّتَ اللهُ قَدَمَيْهِ يَوْمَ تَزُولُ فِيهِ الْجِبَالُ»

*"If one helps his brother in need, Allâh makes his feet firm
on the day during which the mountains will perish."*[3]

Nauful bin Mu'âwiyah ﷺ performed *Hajj* for a second time
in the year 10 H, this time with the Prophet ﷺ during his
Farewell Pilgrimage.

---

[1] *Al-Majma'* 10/ 221 from Al-Bazzar.
[2] Reported by Ibn Abi Ad-Dunya in *Qadha'il-Hawa'ij* 49 from Hasan.
[3] *Ibn An-Najjar* 5/126 from Abdullah bin 'Abbas and *Sahihul-Jami'* 176.

During the Caliphate of 'Umar bin Al-Khattâb ☙

When the Leader of the Believers, 'Umar bin Al-Khattâb ☙, marched towards Ash-Sham (Syria and surrounding regions, such as Palestine), Nawful bin Mu'âwiyah ☙ was one of the Companions ☙ who went with him.

One day, 'Uyainah bin Hisn bin Hudhaifah bin Badr went to meet his nephew, Al-Hurr bin Qais bin Hisn. Now, it is important to point out that 'Umar ☙ would fill his gatherings with scholars and people who were knowledgeable about the Qur'ân, regardless of whether they were old or young. Al-Hurr bin Qais was one of those people, and so 'Uyainah asked him if he could help him meet the Khalifah. Al-Hurr promised to arrange the meeting for his uncle.

Later on, while 'Umar ☙ was sitting down with Naufal bin Mu'âwiyah ☙ and discussing with him the events that took place years earlier during the siege of Tâ'if, Al-Hurr presented himself and asked for permission to enter on behalf of his uncle, 'Uyainah.

'Uyainah then entered and said, "O son of Al-Khattâb, by Allâh, you do not give us generously, and you do not rule among us justly." When Naufal bin Mu'âwiyah ☙ saw the anger on 'Umar's face, he feared that something serious was going to happen, but Al-Hurr bin Qais was quick to ease the tension. He said, "O Leader of the Believers, verily, Allâh ☙ said to His Prophet ﷺ:

$$﴿ خُذِ ٱلْعَفْوَ وَأْمُرْ بِٱلْعُرْفِ وَأَعْرِضْ عَنِ ٱلْجَٰهِلِينَ ١٩٩ ﴾$$

"Show forgiveness, enjoin what is good, and turn away from the foolish (i.e., don't punish them)."[1]

---

[1] *Qur'ân* 7: 199 and see *Al-Bukhari* 4642 and others.

And as was always the case, 'Umar ☙ submitted to the ruling he found in Allâh's Book.

His Death

It is for the most part held that Naufal bin Mu'âwiyah Ad-Dili ☙ lived until the ripe age of one-hundred and twenty, sixty years of which he lived as a non-Muslim, and the other sixty as a Muslim. But it has also been said that he died when he was 100 years old. Naufal bin Mu'âwiyah ☙ died in Al-Madinah during the rule of Yazid bin Mu'âwiyah (apparently, there is no relation between the two).

A Narrator of the Prophet's *Ahâdith*

Abu Bakr bin 'Abdur-Rahmân bin Al-Hârith bin Hishâm, 'Abdur-Rahmân bin Muti' bin Al-Aswad, and 'Irâk bin Mâlik – each of these three related *Hadith* narrations from Naufal bin Mu'âwiyah Ad-Dili ☙.

Sa‘d bin ‘Ubâdah ﷺ

Sa'd bin 'Ubâdah ﷺ

His Lineage

He is Sa'd bin 'Ubâdah bin Dulaim – it has also been said: Ibn Abi Hazimah – bin Hârithah bin Harâm bin Tha'labah bin Tarif bin Al-Khazraj. He ﷺ was the chief of Khazjraj, one of the two tribes of Al-Madinah. And his mother was 'Amrah bint Mas'ûd.

His *Kunyah*

His *Kunyah* was Abu Thâbit, but he was also sometimes referred to as Abu Qais.

Before Islam

Even before the advent of Islam, Sa'd bin 'Ubâdah ﷺ was literate: he was able to write in Arabic. This was something of a feat at the time because most Arabs were illiterate. He was also a skilled swimmer and archer.

His Islam

Sa'd bin 'Ubâdah ﷺ was one of the first to embrace Islam in Al-Madinah. Representing the Banu Sâ'idah clan along with Al-Mundhir bin 'Amr ﷺ, Sa'd ﷺ pledged allegiance to the

Prophet ﷺ on the Day of Al-'Aqabah.

Tortured for his Beliefs

It was not uncommon for a Muslim from Makkah to endure torture at the hands of the polytheists. Almost every Muslim living in Makkah had to endure some form of physical torture or punishment, but not so for the dwellers of Al-Madinah. Once the Pledge of Al-'Aqabah was made, Islam spread very rapidly in Al-Madinah; furthermore, whereas most of Makkah's elite rejected Islam, most of Al-Madinah's elite raced to embrace it.

Therefore, no one in Al-Madinah was ever persecuted by the Quraish for being a Muslim, that is, with one exception – Sa'd bin 'Ubâdah ﷺ. Under normal circumstances, the Quraish would not dare to inflict harm upon Sa'd ﷺ. He was the leader of the Khazraj tribe, which made harming him dangerous to the Quraish, since their trading caravans had to pass through Al-Madinah. So if they harmed him, the fellow tribesmen of Sa'd ﷺ would have the opportunity of exacting revenge every time a trading caravan of the Quraish passed through Al-Madinah.

Nonetheless, the Quraish did end up inflicting physical harm upon Sa'd ﷺ, making him the sole person from the *Ansâr* to endure punishment at their hands. When the Pledge of Al-'Aqabah was completed, the people could clearly hear the sound of a loud voice emanating from the peak of the mountain: "O people of Quraish, here are the sons of Al-'Aus and Al-Khazraj becoming allies in order to fight you."

Upon hearing this voice, the delegates from Al-Madinah were at first terrified, but then the Prophet ﷺ calmed their nerves by saying, "Do not be frightened by this voice."

Al-'Abbâs bin Nadlah ﷺ said to the Messenger of Allâh ﷺ, "By the One Who has sent you with the truth, if you wish, we will lean upon the people of Mina (the Quraish) tomorrow with our swords (i.e., we will fight them)."

«لَمْ أُومَرْ بِذَلِكَ، وَلَكِنْ ارْجِعُوا إِلَى رِحَالِكُمْ»

"I have not been commanded to do that," answered the Prophet ﷺ. *"Instead, return to your camp (the place they were staying during their sojourn in Makkah)."*

When the leaders of the Quraish found out that the people of Al-Madinah had pledged allegiance to the Prophet ﷺ, had agreed to welcome him in their homeland, and had promised to defend him, they became filled with rage. Led by Abu Jahl, the leaders of the Quraish headed out towards the encampment of the visitors from Yathrib, but they were too late; the delegates had already left. Their anger had to be quenched, however, and so they followed the trail of the delegates. Most were already beyond the reach of the Quraish, but Sa'd bin 'Ubâdah ﷺ and Mundhir bin 'Amr ﷺ were delayed by business in Makkah, and so the Quraish were able to catch up to them. As for Al-Mundhir ﷺ, he was able to escape. But Sa'd ﷺ was taken captive.

Quraish's leaders first tied Sa'd's hands behind his neck. Then they began to hit him violently on his face, only stopping to drag him by his thick hair until they returned to Makkah. Sa'd ﷺ later recounted what happened when he entered Makkah: "While I was with the people, being dealt with blows, a tall, handsome man with a white, radiant face appeared before me. I thought to myself, 'If just one of these people has any goodness in him, he must be that man.'" But when that man drew near, he delivered a violent punch to Sa'd's body. At that point, Sa'd ﷺ said to himself, "By Allâh, after this, (I knew that) there is no goodness in them." The man with the white, radiant face was Suhail bin 'Amr.

Abul-Bakhtari bin Hishâm was shocked to see how harshly Sa'd bin 'Ubâdah ﷺ was being treated; perhaps he also sensed the danger of beating up on someone who was so important, someone who could potentially wreak havoc on Quraish's trade routes. Either the Quraish didn't know whom it was they were beating; or they knew, but didn't care because they were in a state of extreme anger.

Abul-Bakhtari did know who Sa'd ﷺ was, and as quickly as he could, he raced to Sa'd ﷺ and whispered into his ear, "Woe unto you! Is there no one from the Quraish with whom you have a covenant or an allegiance?"

Hardly able to keep himself up, Sa'd ﷺ answered in a tired voice, "Yes, I was a hired worker of Jubair bin Mut'im and of Al-Harth bin Umayyah. I would protect their business (caravans) from anyone who wanted to harm them in my lands."

"Woe unto you!" exclaimed Abul-Bakhtari. "Call out their names!"

"O Jubair bin Mut'im! O Al-Harth bin Harb!" called out Sa'd ﷺ. Abul-Bakhtari sprang into action, running towards Jubair and Harth, and saying to them when he found them, "Indeed, a man from the Khazraj is being beaten, and he is calling out your names."

"Who is he?" asked Jubair and Al-Harth.

"Verily, he is Sa'd bin 'Ubâdah," answered Abul-Bakhtari. They of course immediately recognized his name, and no sooner did they hear it than they raced towards Sa'd ﷺ in order to grant him protection and save him from the hands of the Quraish. As soon as Sa'd ❀ gained their protection, he hurried to catch up with his fellow delegates from the *Ansâr*, who were already well on their way back to Al-Madinah.

Sa'd's Generosity

There was a tradition of generosity in Sa'd's family: He, like his forefathers before him, would call out every day, "Whoever loves grease and meat, then let him come to the (serving) dish of Dulaim bin Hârithah (the name of Sa'd's grandfather)." Sa'd's serving tray would follow the Prophet ﷺ in the houses of the Prophet's wives.

The people of *Suffah* were poor Companions ❀ who had no homes of their own and so slept in the Prophet's *Masjid*. The Prophet ﷺ would encourage his Companions ❀ to share their food with them. Some would share their food with one or two people; others shared with more; as for Sa'd bin 'Ubâdah ❀, he would share his dinner with 80 men from the people of *Suffah*.

The Banner of the Messenger of Allâh ﷺ

The Prophet ﷺ had at least two banners, one with 'Ali bin Abi Tâlib ❀, and it was the banner of the *Muhâjirûn*; and the other, the banner of the *Ansâr*, with Sa'd bin 'Ubâdah ❀.

The Prophet ﷺ Consults Sa'd bin 'Ubâdah ❀ on the Day of Khandaq

The Prophet ﷺ had many Companions ❀. So out of those many Companions, if it is related in a *Hadith* that he consulted with one of them in particular, we can know for certain that a great honor was being bestowed on that Companions ﷺ; and Sa'd bin 'Ubâdah ﷺ was one such Companion. When the Prophet ﷺ learned about the coming of the Confederate armies, he ﷺ consulted Sa'd ﷺ, asking him whether it was better to go out and meet the enemy or to wait until the enemy came to them in Al-Madinah.

Sa'd bin 'Ubâdah ﷺ and Banu Quraizah

When the Prophet ﷺ arrived in Al-Madinah, three Jewish tribes were among its inhabitants, with the rest of its inhabitants belonging either to the 'Aus or Khazraj tribe. It was the members of the 'Aus and Khazraj tribes who pledged allegiance to the Prophet ﷺ and promised to defend him, and so the Prophet's initial dealings with the other tribes of Al-Madinah were crucial to the stability of the new Muslim country.

Upon arriving in Al-Madinah, the Prophet ﷺ signed an important treaty with all three Jewish tribes. The main part of the treaty was that if anyone attacked any of the Jewish tribes, the Muslims had to defend them; and that if anyone attacked the Muslims, the three Jewish tribes had to defend them.

One day, the Messenger of Allâh ﷺ went to No'mân bin Adâ, Bahrâ bin 'Amr, and Shâsh bin 'Adi, three Jews. He ﷺ invited them to Islam and warned them about Allâh's punishment. They answered, "What are you frightening us about, O Muhammad? We are the sons of Allâh and His loved ones." This claim was similar to the one that the Christians made.

Allâh ﷺ then revealed the Verse:

﴿وَقَالَتِ ٱلۡيَهُودُ وَٱلنَّصَٰرَىٰ نَحۡنُ أَبۡنَٰٓؤُاْ ٱللَّهِ وَأَحِبَّٰٓؤُهُۥ قُلۡ فَلِمَ يُعَذِّبُكُم﴾

بِذُنُوبِكُم بَلْ أَنتُم بَشَرٌ مِّمَّنْ خَلَقَ ﴾

"And (both) the Jews and the Christians say: "We are the children of Allâh and His loved ones." Say: "Why then does He punish you for your sins?" Nay, you are but human beings, of those He has created."[1]

Sa'd bin 'Ubâdah, Mu'âdh bin Jabal, and 'Uqbah bin Wahb ۞ – these three Companions ۞ said, "O group of Jews: Fear Allâh. For by Allâh, you indeed know that he is the Messenger of Allâh. You used to remind us about him before he was sent, and you used to describe him with his exact description."

Râfi' bin Huraimalah and Wahb bin Yahûdha answered, "We never said that to you, and Allâh never revealed a book after the time of Mûsa, nor did He send a bearer of glad tidings or a warner after him (i.e., after Mûsa ۞)." Allâh ۞ then revealed the Verse:

﴿ يَـٰٓأَهْلَ ٱلْكِتَـٰبِ قَدْ جَآءَكُمْ رَسُولُنَا يُبَيِّنُ لَكُمْ عَلَىٰ فَتْرَةٍ مِّنَ ٱلرُّسُلِ أَن تَقُولُوا۟ مَا جَآءَنَا مِنۢ بَشِيرٍ وَلَا نَذِيرٍ فَقَدْ جَآءَكُم بَشِيرٌ وَنَذِيرٌ وَٱللَّهُ عَلَىٰ كُلِّ شَىْءٍ قَدِيرٌ ۝ ﴾

"O people of the Scripture (Jews and Christians)! Now has come to you Our Messenger (Muhammad ۞) making (things) clear unto you, after a break in (the series of) Messengers, lest you say: "There came unto us no bringer of glad tidings and no warner." But now has come unto you a bringer of glad tidings and a warner. And Allâh is Able to do all things."[2]

---

[1] *Qur'ân* 5: 18.
[2] *Qur'ân* 5: 19, and see *At-Tabari* 11616.

When the confederate armies threatened the Muslims from the northern front of Al-Madinah, the Muslims felt safe from the southern front for many reasons, one of them being that their allies, the members of the Banu Quraizah tribe, lived in southern Al-Madinah. Consider, then, the Muslims' anger when they heard that Banu Quraizah was violating its pact and was helping the confederate armies against the Muslims.

The Prophet ﷺ wanted to be sure, so he sent a number of Companions ﷺ to ascertain whether Banu Quraizah was really betraying them. The Companions ﷺ he ﷺ sent were Sa'd bin 'Ubâdah ﷺ, the leader of Khazraj; Sa'd bin Mu'âdh ﷺ, the leader of 'Aus; 'Abdullâh bin Rawâhah ﷺ; Khawwât bin Jubair ﷺ; and Usaid bin Hudair ﷺ.

Soon, it became clear that Banu Quraizah broke the pact it made with the Muslims and was helping the confederate armies. Also, the hypocrites openly displayed their true colors. Both Banu Quraizah and the hypocrites showed open enmity to the Prophet ﷺ because they felt certain that, with 12,000 fighters waiting to enter Al-Madinah, the odds were stacked heavily against the Muslims. A solution had to be found for all of these problems, and so the Prophet ﷺ sent for 'Uyainah bin Hisn Al-Fazâri and Al-Harth bin 'Auf.

'Uyainah and Al-Harth were from one of the tribes that came to fight the Muslims. The Prophet ﷺ offered them one-third of Al-Madinah's crops if they left immediately with their people. One-third was a heavy price to pay, but the Muslims stood a better chance of winning the battle if there was going to be fewer opponents. 'Uyainah and Al-Harth, who came secretly so that Abu Sufyân wouldn't see them, asked for one-half of Al-Madinah's harvest. When they realized that the Prophet ﷺ was not going to agree to more than one-third, they accepted his terms. However, before signing the agreement, the Prophet 🙵 wanted to consult Sa'd bin 'Ubâdah 🙵 and Sa'd bin Mu'âdh 🙵.

"O Messenger of Allâh," said Sa'd bin 'Ubâdah 🙵 after he heard about the deal from the Prophet 🙵, "is this (i.e., this agreement) something you love, so that we will then do it (because we know you love it)? Or is this something that Allâh commanded you with, so that we must act accordingly? Or is this something that you are doing for us (so that we have the option to give our opinion in the matter)?"

"Had Allâh commanded me (to do this), I would not have consulted you both," said the Prophet 🙵. "By Allâh, I did this (i.e., I called them here to negotiate terms with them) only because I saw that the Arabs have fired at you from a single bow, and they have (joined to) show you enmity from all directions...."

"Then they will have nothing from us other than the sword," said Sa'd bin 'Ubâdah 🙵.

"Then that is your choice [and it will be executed (i.e., I accept your choice)]," said the Prophet 🙵.

The Prophet 🙵 then returned to 'Uyainah and Al-Harth, and said, "Return, for between us and you is the sword."

The People of *Suffah*

As I mentioned earlier, the People of *Suffah* were poor Companions who lived in the Prophet's *Masjid* since they had no homes of their own. Most of these people were from the *Muhâjirûn*, who, when they migrated to Al-Madinah, had left behind all of their wealth in Makkah. When it was dinnertime, well-off Muslims would share their meals with these poor Muslims. Some entertained one poor person; others, two; and yet others, more. As for Sa'd bin 'Ubâdah ⬥, he would take eighty men from the People of *Suffah* back with him to his home and share his food with them.

The Death of 'Amrah bint Mas'ûd ⬥

While Sa'd bin 'Ubâdah ⬥ was away on a mission to Daumatul-Jandal in the year 5 H, his mother, 'Amrah bint Mas'ûd ⬥, died. When the Messenger of Allâh ﷺ returned, he performed prayer over her. Then Sa'd ⬥ approached him and said, "O Messenger of Allâh, my mother died while I was away from her. Will it do her any good if I give charity on her behalf?." "Yes," said the Prophet ﷺ.

"Then indeed, I make you bear witness that I give my garden ... away to charity on her behalf," said Sa'd ⬥. "O Messenger of Allâh, my mother died without having bequeathed anything (for charity). Will it do her any good if I give charity on her behalf?"

"Yes," said the Messenger of Allâh ﷺ.

"And which charity is most beloved to you?"

"Provide (people with) drink (for example, by carrying water to people, by providing people with the tools they need to dig wells and to draw water from wells, etc.)," said the Prophet ﷺ. This advice is most timely indeed: Whereas many of us, by the grace of Allâh ﷻ, have a seemingly unlimited supply of running water, many of our brothers and sisters in Africa and elsewhere have a hard time finding clean drinking water. Muslims therefore need to dedicate their expertise and resources to helping their brothers and sisters in finding and digging wells in areas wherein there is a lack of clean water. That the Prophet ﷺ told Sa'd ⬥ to provide drinking water as a way of giving charity on behalf of his mother proves that it is one of the best deeds that a person can do.

"And Peace be upon You, O Messenger of Allâh"

Once, when the Messenger of Allâh 攤 came to the door of Sa'd's home, he 攤 said, "May peace and the mercy of Allâh be upon you." Both Sa'd ﷺ and his son, Qais ﷺ, clearly heard the Prophet's greeting, but Sa'd ﷺ did not respond. Then for a second time the Prophet 攤 said, "May Peace and the Mercy of Allâh be upon you." Sa'd ﷺ whispered an answer, clearly not in a loud enough tone for the Prophet 攤 to hear him.

"Will you not give the Messenger of Allâh 攤 permission to enter?" asked Qais ﷺ, somewhat shocked at his father's seemingly strange behavior.

"Let him send many greetings of peace upon us," answered Sa'd ﷺ. This was Sa'd's only motive: he wanted to gain as much blessings as possible, and he knew that each greeting of peace that emanated from the Messenger of Allâh 攤 was blessed.

The Messenger of Allâh 攤 then stopped knocking and went away. When Sa'd ﷺ heard no more greetings from outside of his door, he raced outside until he caught up with the Messenger of Allâh 攤. And when he did, he ﷺ said, "And peace be upon you, O Messenger of Allâh. All that I wanted was for you to send a great many greetings of peace (upon me and my family). By Allâh, I had heard you (all along)." The Messenger of Allâh 攤 then walked back with Sa'd ﷺ until he entered his house.

Sending Prayers upon the Prophet ﷺ

Abu Mas'ûd Al-Ansâri ﷺ said, "We once went to the Messenger of Allâh ﷺ, and together we then sat in the gathering (perhaps here meaning home) of Sa'd bin 'Ubâdah ﷺ. Bashir bin Sa'd ﷺ said (to the Prophet ﷺ), 'We have been ordered to send prayers upon you, O Messenger of Allâh. So how can we go about sending prayers upon you?' At first, the Messenger of Allâh ﷺ remained silent, and then he continued to do so until Bashir bin Sa'd ﷺ wished that he had never asked him (that question). Finally, the Messenger of Allâh ﷺ said:

«قُولُوا : اللَّهُمَّ صَلِّ عَلَى مُحَمَّدٍ وَعَلَى آلِ مُحَمَّدٍ كَمَا صَلَّيْتَ عَلَى إِبْرَاهِيمَ، وَبَارِكْ عَلَى مُحَمَّدٍ وَعَلَى آلِ مُحَمَّدٍ، كَمَا بَارَكْتَ عَلَى إِبْرَاهِيمَ وَعَلَى آلِ إِبْرَاهِيمَ فِي الْعَالَمِينَ إِنَّكَ حَمِيدٌ مَجِيدٌ»

Say: 'O Allâh, send prayers (i.e., praise and exalt him in the highest and most superior of gatherings: that of the closest angels to Allâh) upon Muhammad and the followers (some scholars are of the view that the meaning here is more specific than 'followers,' or more precisely, his ﷺ followers from among his family) of Muhammad, just as You sent prayers upon Ibrahim; and send blessings upon Muhammad and upon the family of Muhammad, just as You sent blessings upon Ibrahim and upon the family of Ibraheem among the 'Alâmin (all that exists). Verily, You are full of praise and majesty.'[1]

---

[1] *An-Nasai* 286 and *Abu Dâwud* 980.

The Day of the Makkah Conquest

On the day that the Muslims conquered Makkah, the Messenger of Allâh's banner was with Sa'd bin 'Ubâdah 🌸. When Sa'd 🌸, with banner in hand, passed by Abu Sufyân 🌸, he said, "Today is the Day of Slaughter. Today, the sanctity (of Makkah) will be made lawful (i.e., although fighting is forbidden in Makkah, an exception will be made today). Today, Allâh will humiliate the Quraish." Sa'd 🌸 was speaking from the heart and with a great deal of zeal; he could not forget the many years that the Quraish had waged war against the Prophet 🌸. Nonetheless, he was addressing a man who had just recently embraced Islam and who was hoping that the Prophet 🌸 would have mercy on his people. And so when the Messenger of Allâh 🌸 passed by him, Abu Sufyân 🌸 called out, "O Messenger of Allâh, have you been ordered to fight your own people? For indeed, when Sa'd 🌸 and those with him passed by us, he claimed that he will fight us. He said, 'Today is the Day of Slaughter, today the sanctity (of Makkah) will be made lawful, today Allâh will humiliate the Quraish. I indeed ask you, by Allâh, to be good to your people, for you are the most faithful of people, the most merciful of people, and the kindest of people (to his relatives, fellow tribesmen, etc.)."

'Uthmân bin 'Affân 🌸 and 'Abdur-Rahmân bin 'Auf 🌸 then told the Prophet 🌸 that they feared that, through his zeal, Sa'd 🌸 would start fighting against the Quraish. In order to allay everyone's fears, the Messenger of Allâh 🌸 said:

«لَا يَا أَبَا سُفْيَانَ، الْيَوْمُ يَوْمُ الْمَرْحَمَةِ، الْيَوْمَ أَعَزَّ اللهُ قُرَيْشًا»

"No, O Abu Sufyân, today is the day of mercy. Today, Allâh will bestow honor upon the Quraish."

The Messenger of Allâh ﷺ sent orders to the vanguard of his army; and by dint of those orders, the banner was removed from the hand of Sa'd bin 'Ubâdah ؓ and was instead placed in the hand of his son, Qais ؓ. This way, everyone was appeased and no one's feelings were hurt. Now that the banner was in someone else's hand, Abu Sufyân ؓ had no further cause to be afraid. And Sa'd's feelings were preserved, for it was just as great an honor to Sa'd ؓ for his son to carry the banner of the Messenger of Allâh ﷺ.

The Roofed Shelter of Banu Sâ'idah

Just after the Prophet ﷺ died, the *Ansâr* gathered in a place that was known as the roofed shelter of the Banu Sâ'idah clan. They met to choose a leader from among them. The *Muhâjirûn* were excluded from this meeting on purpose, for at first the *Ansâr* felt that it was their right that the leader of the Muslims should be chosen from among them. And so it came as no surprise when they decided that Sa'd bin 'Ubâdah ؓ, chief of the Khazraj tribe, should be their next leader. This decision was of course incorrect, for although Sa'd ؓ was a noble and pious Muslim, there were others, from the *Muhâjirûn*, who were more worthy than he of becoming *Khalifah*.

Abu Bakr ؓ, 'Umar ؓ, and others from the *Muhâjirûn* heard about the meeting and went to it. A brief discussion ensued, during which the *Muhâjirûn* made it clear that it was their proper role to be leaders and that it was the *Ansâr*'s proper role to be their ministers. Therefore, a leader must be chosen from the *Muhâjirûn*. In the end, 'Umar ؓ said to Abu Bakr ؓ, "Extend your hand, and I will pledge allegiance to you." Abu Bakr ؓ was reluctant, but things happened so quickly that he hardly had time to respond, for as soon as 'Umar ؓ pledged allegiance to him, everyone else followed suit. It was of course the best decision, for the Prophet 🙵 had, on more than one occasion, alluded to the fact that Abu Bakr 🙵 should be the *Khalifah* after him.

Sa'd's Death

Sa'd bin 'Ubâdah 🙵 died in Basrah; however, there are conflicting views in the matter. Some say that he died during the caliphate of 'Umar bin Al-Khattâb 🙵 and was buried in the land of Hawrân. Others say that his grave is in Al-Manihah, which is one of the villages of Damascus.

Mâlik bin Sinân رضي الله عنه

Mâlik bin Sinân ﷺ

His Lineage

He is Mâlik bin Sinân bin Tha'labah bin Al-Abhar (Khudrah bin 'Auf) bin Al-Hârith bin Al-Khazraj.

His *Kunyah*

His *Kunyah* is Abu (father of) Sa'id, for he ﷺ is the father of Abu Sa'id Al-Khudri ﷺ.

His Islam

Mâlik bin Sinân ﷺ embraced Islam shortly after the famous Pledge of Al-'Aqabah.

The Changing of the *Qiblah*

At first, the Muslims prayed towards Jerusalem. But then, eighteen months after the Messenger of Allâh ﷺ arrived in Al-Madinah, the new *Qiblah* (place towards which one turns when one performs prayer) of the Muslims became the Ka'bah in Makkah. Mâlik bin Sinân ﷺ said, "The *Qiblah* was changed halfway through Sha'bân, at the beginning of the eighteenth month after the *Hijrah* (migration of the Prophet ﷺ to Al-Madinah)."

Al-Barâ' bin 'Azib ﷺ said, "The Messenger of Allâh ﷺ prayed towards Jerusalem for 16 or 17 months (after his arrival in Al-Madinah). But (throughout that time) he longed to be ordered to face the Ka'bah. Then Allâh ﷻ revealed the Verse:

﴿قَدْ نَرَىٰ تَقَلُّبَ وَجْهِكَ فِي ٱلسَّمَآءِ فَلَنُوَلِّيَنَّكَ قِبْلَةً تَرْضَىٰهَا فَوَلِّ وَجْهَكَ شَطْرَ ٱلْمَسْجِدِ ٱلْحَرَامِ﴾

"Verily! We have seen the turning of your (Muhammad's ﷺ) face towards the heaven. Surely, We shall turn you to a Qiblah (prayer direction) that shall please you, so turn your face in the direction of Al-Masjid-al-Haram (at Makkah)."[1]

Mâlik bin Sinân ﷺ said that, when the Messenger of Allâh ﷺ was ordered to face the Ka'bah (during prayer), the *Qiblah* of Ibrâhîm ﷺ, the Jews became angry and said, "What about those who used to pray towards our *Qiblah* (Jerusalem)?" They were referring to the Muslims that had died before their *Qiblah* was changed, and so they were insinuating that those Muslims would not be rewarded for their prayers.

And so a number of Companions ﷺ, among whom was Mâlik bin Sinân ﷺ and Bishr bin Al-Barâ' ﷺ, went to the Prophet ﷺ and said, "O Messenger of Allâh, what about our brothers who have died – Al-Barâ' bin Ma'rûr ﷺ, As'ad bin Zurârah, and 'Uthmân bin Maz'ûn ﷺ – and who used to pray facing Jerusalem?"

In answer to their question, the following Verse was then revealed:

﴿وَمَا كَانَ ٱللَّهُ لِيُضِيعَ إِيمَٰنَكُمْ﴾

"And Allâh would never make your faith (prayers) to be

---

[1] *Qur'ân* 2: 144.

lost (i.e., your prayers offered towards Jerusalem)."[1]

The Day of Uhud

After they suffered a humiliating defeat at the hands of the Muslims on the Day of Badr, the Quraish longed for the day when they would be able to taste the sweetness of revenge. At first, their desire for revenge was mixed with a sense of mourning for their relatives that died during the Battle of Badr. But soon their desire for revenge increased until it finally became an obsession; it was the one constant thought that was on everyone's mind.

Slowly but surely, they made preparations for another assault on Al-Madinah; they did this by earmarking profits they made in trade for purchasing the supplies they needed for the planned attack. When they finally set out for Al-Madinah in the year 3 H, they had managed to put together a formidable army that consisted of 3000 fighters. They had 200 horses as well as 300 camels that were loaded with weapons and supplies. And 700 of their fighters were protected by armor. This time around, the women accompanied the men on their expedition, not to fight but to encourage them, goad them on, and constantly remind them of their relatives that had died during Badr.

After the Messenger of Allâh ﷺ was informed that the Quraish were coming with their army, the Muslims gathered for the Jumu'ah (Friday) prayer; then the Prophet ﷺ stood on the pulpit, praised and extolled Allâh ﷺ, and said:

«أَيُّهَا النَّاسُ إِنِّي قَدْ رَأَيْتُ فِي مَنَامِي رُؤْيَا، رَأَيْتُ كَأَنِّي فِي دِرْعٍ

---

[1] *Qur'ân* 2: 143.

حَصِينَةٍ، وَرَأَيْتُ كَأَنَّ سَيْفِي ذَا الْفَقَارِ انْفَصَمَ مِنْ عِنْدِ ظُبَتِهِ، وَرَأَيْتُ

بَقَرًا تُذْبَحُ، وَرَأَيْتُ كَأَنِّي مُرْدِفٌ كَبْشًا»

"O people, I have indeed seen a dream during my sleep. I saw that it was as if I were in impenetrable armor. And I saw that it was as if my sword, Dhal-Faqar (the name of his sword), shattered from the edge of its blade. I also saw a cow being slaughtered. And I saw that it was as if I were seated behind (a rider) on a ram."

His Companions ﷺ asked, "O Messenger of Allâh, how have you interpreted it?" He ﷺ said:

«أَمَّا الدِّرْعُ الْحَصِينَةُ فَالْمَدِينَةُ، وَأَمَّا انْفِصَامُ سَيْفِي فَقَتْلُ رَجُلٍ مِنْ أَهْلِ بَيْتِي، وَأَمَّا الْبَقَرُ الْمُذَبَّحُ فَقَتْلِى فِي أَصْحَابِي، وَأَمَّا أَنِّي مُرْدِفٌ كَبْشًا فَكَبْشُ الْكَتِيبَةِ - حَامِلُ لِوَاءِ الْمُشْرِكِينَ - نَقْتُلُهُ إِنْ شَاءَ اللهُ»

"As for the impenetrable armor, it is Al-Madinah (i.e., they would be safe by staying in Madinah instead of going out to meet the oncoming army). As for the shattering of my sword, then it is the killing of a man from the people of my household. As for the slaughtered cow, it is some of my Companions being killed. And as for me sitting behind (a rider on) a ram, it is the ram of the fighters – the bearer of the polytheists' banner – we will kill him, by the will of Allâh."[1]

Upon the completion of the Friday prayer, the *Muhâjirûn* and the *Ansâr* surrounded the Messenger of Allâh ﷺ, and he ﷺ said to them, "Give me your counsel." The Prophet ﷺ, perhaps based mainly on his dream, felt that it was best to

---

[1] *Al-Waqidi* 209, 247, and *Ahmad* 1/271.

stay in Al-Madinah. He ﷺ said:

«امْكُثُوا فِي الْمَدِينَةِ وَاجْعَلُوا النِّسَاءَ وَالذَّرَارِيَّ فِي الآطَامِ، فَإِنْ دُخِلَ عَلَيْنَا قَاتَلْنَاهُمْ فِي الأَزِقَّةِ، فَنَحْنُ أَعْلَمُ بِهَا مِنْهُمْ، وَرُمُوا مِنْ فَوْقِ الصِّيَاصِي وَالآطَامِ»

"Remain in Al-Madinah, and place your women and children on the top of high buildings. If they (the enemy) enter upon us, we will fight them in the narrow roads, for we are better acquainted with those roads than they are. And they can be shot at (with arrows) from... the tops of high buildings."

However, many young men who had missed the Battle of Badr were eager to go out and meet the enemy, and so they pleaded with the Prophet ﷺ, saying, "Take us out to our enemy." Agreeing with them, but for other reasons, were some of the more wise and aged Muslims from the *Muhâjirûn* and the *Ansâr* – such as Hamzah bin 'Abdul-Muttalib ﷺ, Sa'd bin 'Ubâdah ﷺ, Mâlik bin Sinân ﷺ, and An-No'mân bin Mâlik ﷺ. They all echoed the same opinion:

O Messenger of Allâh, we indeed fear that the enemy will think that we are cowards if we do not go out to meet them, and that they will then become bold against us. On the Day of Badr, we were 300 men, and Allâh made you victorious through them. And today, we are many people, and we were (long) hoping for this day and supplicating for it. And Allâh has indeed brought it to us in this arena of ours.

Mâlik bin Sinân ﷺ said, "O Messenger of Allâh, by Allâh, we are facing one of two good outcomes. Either Allâh will grant us victory over them, which is what we want, and Allâh ﷻ will humiliate them, as happened on the Day of

Badr, so that (after they are destroyed) only wanderers among them will remain. Or, O Messenger of Allâh, Allâh will grant us martyrdom. O Messenger of Allâh, by Allâh, we do not mind which of the two possible outcomes actually takes place, for both of them are good."

When he ﷺ saw that the view of so many seemed to be in favor of going out to meet the enemy, the Prophet ﷺ said, "I indeed fear that you will face defeat." But still, they insisted upon going out. The Prophet ﷺ let the matter rest, and instead began admonishing them and advising them to be strong and steadfast in battle. He informed them that, as long as they remained patient, they would come out as victors. And the people then became overjoyed when the Prophet ﷺ told them that they were going to go out to meet the enemy.

Taking with him Abu Bakr ﷺ and 'Umar ﷺ, the Messenger of Allâh ﷺ entered his home. His two closest Companions ﷺ then helped him don his armor for battle. Meanwhile, the Muslims stood outside in rows, waiting for him to come out. While they were waiting, Sa'd bin Mu'âdh ﷺ and Usaid bin Hudair ﷺ approached them and said, "You know very well what you said to the Messenger of Allâh ﷺ. You pressured him to go out even though the matter (i.e., revelation) descends to him from the sky. Let him decide (what you should do). Whatever he commands you to do, do it."

The other Companions ﷺ began to feel that they had done wrong in pleading too much with the Prophet ﷺ, and so, when the Prophet ﷺ came out, they apologized and suggested that they should stay in Al-Madinah. By then, however, the Prophet ﷺ had already donned his armor, and he made it clear to them that, when a Prophet ﷺ dons his armor to meet the enemy, there is no turning back, but rather he goes forth, waiting for Allâh's Decision between him and his enemies.

Accompanied by 1000 of his Companions 🌺, The Messenger of Allâh 🕌 then left for Uhud. Of all the people who had suggested that the Muslims go out and face the enemy, there was one notable dissenter, 'Abdullâh bin Ubai bin Salûl, most commonly referred to as the Chief of the Hypocrites. He displayed a great deal of anger when he found out that the Prophet 🕌 rejected his advice and accepted the advice of the others. I use the word 'displayed' because he wasn't really angry; he was simply looking for an excuse to cause panic among the ranks of the Muslim army. He told many of his followers that, since the Prophet 🕌 didn't accept his advice, they should all return to Al-Madinah. He said, "He (i.e., the Prophet 🕌) obeyed them and disobeyed me, so I do not know why we should kill ourselves (by going out to fight with him)." Then, led by Ibn Ubai, 300 men from the people of hypocrisy and doubt withdrew from the Muslim army and returned to Al-Madinah. 'Abdullâh bin 'Amr bin Harâm 🌺 and Mâlik bin Sinân 🌺 went after them to remind them about the vile nature of their action. 'Abdullâh 🌺 said, "I remind you about Allâh, your religion, your Prophet, and the pledge you made to protect him (the Prophet 🕌) just as you protect yourselves, your children, and your wives."

"We would have protected him in our city," said Ibn Ubai. "But he has opposed us. I advised him but he refused to take my advice, and instead decided to obey the views of children."

When Ibn Ubai and his followers continued their march back towards Al-Madinah, 'Abdullâh and Mâlik bin Sinân 🌺 called out to them, "May Allâh distance you (from His mercy). Indeed Allâh will save the Prophet and the believers from needing your help."

After disappearance of the hypocrites, the Muslims continued their march until they reached Mount Uhud. Once there, the Messenger of Allâh ﷺ set up his Companions ؠ in rows and informed everyone about their assigned posts for the upcoming battle. The Muslims had the advantage of arriving early at the battlefield, and the Prophet ﷺ intended to use that advantage to the utmost. An integral part of his strategy was to place archers on a small mountain near Mount Uhud. The role of these archers was to prevent the enemy from attacking the Muslims from the rear of their army. No horseman or group of horsemen would dare to go around the mountain when they saw archers perched on top of it, ready to fire at anyone who attempted to pass by them. If the archers did their duty, the Muslims would only have to face the enemy from one front. And because the placement of the archers was so crucial to the outcome of the battle, the Prophet ﷺ gave them clear instructions that they were not to leave their posts, regardless of what they saw on the battlefield – regardless of whether the Muslims were winning or losing.

When the Quraish arrived and the two armies faced each other, the first order of business was, as usual, for a few duels to take place between individual before the actual battle. The bearer of Quraish's banner, Talhah bin Abi Talhah, was the first to come forward and demand that someone from the Muslim army come out to face him in a duel. And we must remember that the Prophet ﷺ saw a dream which indicated that the bearer of Quraish's banner was going to be killed.

No immediate response came from any of the Muslims, so Talhah bin Abi Talhah took the opportunity of the pause to taunt his enemies. He said, "O Companions of Muhammad, you claim that your dead ones go to Paradise and our dead ones go to Hell. So will any of you hasten me to the Hellfire with his sword, or give me the opportunity of hastening him to Paradise with my sword? By Al-Lât and Al-'Uzza (two of the idols that the Quraish worshipped), you have lied. Had you known (and believed) that what you say is true, some of you would have come out to face me."

Someone did go out to face him then – 'Ali bin Abu Tâlib 🍃, who was much younger and less experienced on the battlefield than his opponent. The duel did not last long; as had been requested, 'Ali 🍃 hastened Talhah's journey to the Hellfire with his sword.

"The dream of the Prophet 🍃 has come true," thought Mâlik bin Sinân 🍃. Talhah's brother, 'Uthmân, then came out to engage in a duel. He joined his brother on his journey towards Hell when his opponent, Sa'd bin Abi Waqqâs 🍃, made a direct hit using his bow and arrow.

Then the battle began in earnest, with the polytheists launching an offensive, probably confident with the knowledge that they outnumbered the Muslims at least 3 to 1. But the Muslims, not hampered down by hypocrites, fought valiantly and skillfully as a single unit. Khalid bin Al-Walid, 'Ikrimah bin Abi Jahl, Dirâr bin Al-Khattâb and other horsemen tried to go around the mountain in order to attack the Muslims from behind and to effectively sandwich them from both sides. But when the horsemen tried to pass, the archers from above fired many arrows down at them. The horsemen were therefore forced to retreat; but they decided to wait patiently in the valley, hoping that their strategy would soon pay off.

The rest of Quraish's army was facing an imminent defeat. Their fighters began to flee, as the Muslims raced after them. From the archers' point of view, things were going very well. They saw their fellow Muslims taking prisoners and picking up booty from the battlefield; what's more, they saw the polytheists fleeing from the battlefield. They became very excited and wanted to go down and take their share of the war spoils, but a few of them insisted that they stay, reminding them of the Prophet's orders to stay at their posts, regardless of what happened on the battlefield. Most of them were too excited to heed this advice, so they went down to the battlefield, while only a few of them remained firm on the mountain.

When the horsemen saw them leaving their posts, they knew that their opportunity had come. Khâlid bin Al-Walid and his fellow horsemen attacked the few archers that remained, and then proceeded to launch an attack from the rear of the Muslim army. When the rest of the Quraish saw what was happening, they stopped fleeing and returned to fight. It was now the Muslims who were at a disadvantage.

Many Muslims dropped the booty they had picked up and left the prisoners that were under their care. Added to their difficulty was the problem that they had nowhere to flee as one unit; they were sandwiched in from both sides. Because of the confusion and chaos that ensued, they began to strike one another, thinking that they were fighting the enemy; but then they called out their slogan, so as to avoid striking one another by mistake. They then began to flee in all directions.

Only the Messenger of Allâh ﷺ and a small number of his Companions ﷺ remained firm on the battlefield. Among others, 'Ali bin Abi Tâlib ﷺ, Abu Dujânah ﷺ, Mâlik bin Sinân ﷺ, and Talhah bin 'Ubaidullah ﷺ stayed to fight alongside the Prophet ﷺ. Now that the Prophet ﷺ was vulnerable to attack, the polytheists vowed to kill him.

Here, I am referring to four polytheists in particular: 'Abdullâh bin Shihâb Az-Zuhri, 'Amr bin Qami'ah Al-Laithi, 'Utbah bin Abi Waqqâs, and Safwân bin Umayyah. Even though these four failed in their attempt to kill him, the Prophet ﷺ fell into a hole that was made as a trap by Abu 'Âmir Al-Fâsiq (the wicked-doer). Talhah bin 'Ubaidullah 🙏 embraced the Prophet ﷺ and helped him get back up on his feet. Meanwhile, Mâlik bin Sinân 🙏 sucked and swallowed the blood that covered the Prophet's wound. The Prophet ﷺ said, "Whoever (wishes to) look at a person whose blood is mixed with my blood, then let him took at Mâlik bin Sinân."

Mâlik's Death

When all was said and done after the Battle of Uhud, the Messenger of Allâh ﷺ looked at the martyrs on the battlefield; he ﷺ saw lying in their midst the brave and valiant fighter Mâlik bin Sinân 🙏. The Messenger of Allâh ﷺ said to the families of the martyrs:

«احْفِرُوا وَأَوْسِعُوا وَأَحْسِنُوا، وَادْفِنُوا الِاثْنَيْنِ وَالثَّلَاثَةَ، وَقَدِّمُوا أَكْثَرَهُمْ قُرْآنًا»

"Dig and (dig) wide (graves), and do so nicely. And bury two or three (per grave). And put forward those who knew the most Qur'ân."[1]

---

[1] *Al-Bukhari* 1343, *An-Nasa'i* 2010, 2011 and Albani graded it sound.